ENCOUNTERISM

ENCOUNTERISM

THE NEGLECTED JOYS
OF BEING IN PERSON

ANDY FIELD

W. W. NORTON & COMPANY
Celebrating a Century of Independent Publishing

For information about permission to reproduce selections from this book,
write to Permissions, W. W. Norton & Company, Inc.,
500 Fifth Avenue, New York, NY 10110

For information about special discounts for bulk purchases, please contact
W. W. Norton Special Sales at specialsales@wwnorton.com or 800-233-4830

Manufacturing by Lake Book
Book design by Daniel Lagin
Production manager: Louise Mattarelliano

ISBN 978-1-324-03658-6 (pbk)

W. W. Norton & Company, Inc., 500 Fifth Avenue, New York, N.Y. 10110
www.wwnorton.com

W. W. Norton & Company Ltd., 15 Carlisle Street, London W1D 3BS

1 2 3 4 5 6 7 8 9 0

For BD

How should we take account of, question, describe what happens every day and recurs every day: the banal, the quotidian, the obvious, the common, the ordinary, the infraordinary, the background noise, habitual?

To question the habitual. But that's just it, we're habituated to it.

—GEORGES PEREC,
APPROACHES TO WHAT?

CONTENTS

ABOUT DAZZLEMENT

Like a lot of children, when I was young I was fascinated by all the banal details of the adult world—those little everyday things that my parents and the other adults around me seemed to hardly notice any more. I remember how exciting the idea of a drive-through restaurant was, or going to the hairdresser's. How on holiday we would stand on some foreign street corner and hail a taxi and it would stop just for us. The way car drivers flashed their headlights to say "thank you" to one another and how I could call the receptionist at my dad's office and be transferred right to his desk. Rather than putting on little plays for my family, one of my favourite games was setting up a shopfront at my bedroom door and asking my brother to request various items so that I could go and check if we had them in stock. This adult world, it seemed, was a place of infinite complexity and wonder. A treasure trove of weird rules and routines just waiting to be discovered.

It is hard to retain this excitement as you get older, and to some extent this is probably a good thing. To move through life in a state of relentless wonderment would be both exhausting and time-consuming; stopping to marvel at every vending machine, thrilled anew each day by the process of ordering a coffee. Nonetheless, as an adult I have found it useful to try and keep hold of some of this fascination as a way of drawing my attention back again and again to the parts of the everyday world that often get overlooked.

"We must become preoccupied with and even dazzled by the space and objects of our everyday life, either our bodies, clothes, rooms, or, if need be, the vastness of Forty-second Street," the artist Allan Kaprow once declared, and that dazzlement is what I have spent much of my life chasing. How do we allow ourselves to be amazed by something we encounter every day? How can we approach the world around us with the kind of concentration we normally only reserve for things we deem important or special?

One of the ways I have tried to answer these questions is through the work I make as an artist. I have spent most of the last sixteen years creating unusual performances in everyday locations—in cafés and cinemas, on rooftops, in parks, and out on the crowded streets of towns and cities. Doing so has meant spending a lot of time thinking carefully about these everyday spaces and the kinds of encounters we have in them. Using performance to render the ordinary briefly strange in the hope that doing so might enable people to see it differently.

This book is an extension of that work. It draws from this history of messing around in everyday life to tell stories about a range of ordinary human encounters. The kind of interactions— with hairdressers, nightclubbers, or strangers we pass on the street—that would normally disappear unnoticed into the great ocean of activity occurring around them. Our lives are littered with these encounters. Little interactions occupying a grey space between ritual and routine. Ways of meeting we have grown accustomed to, perhaps even taken for granted.

This book is a story told in nine essays about some of those encounters. Some are encounters with strangers, others with friends and acquaintances. Some happen out in the world and others in places like cinemas and public parks or even on the phone.

Although the idea for this book predates the coronavirus pandemic, much of the writing of it took place in the caesura it created, when most of us found ourselves separated from the activity of our ordinary lives and these familiar encounters were temporarily rendered distant and strange. As the world has opened back up again, I have found myself approaching it with a renewed enthusiasm, ready to be newly dazzled by the wondrous complexity of our interactions with each other.

I hope that you, too, might find yourself dazzled by the nine ordinary encounters I describe here. By writing about them in such detail, I hope to encourage all of us to take greater care over them, and by doing so to take greater care of each other.

ENCOUNTERISM

CHAPTER 1

THE IMPORTANCE OF CARE

In the beginning, there was only hair. Tangled, muddied brambles of hair. Primordial forests of hair. A great, lumpen Pangaea of hair. Hair as far as any eye could bear to see. And then, at some point, there must have been the first haircut. Not hair pulled out from the root in anger or despair, but hair cut deliberately and with some degree of care.

The bare skulls of our earliest ancestors tell us little about the hair on their heads, and although we know humans have used sharp stone tools for hundreds of thousands of years, we don't know if those tools were used for haircutting. What we do have is human remains from as long as twenty-five thousand years ago, and we know that by that time some women wore their hair long in braids whilst some men had theirs cut very short. And by three thousand years ago we have a description of a haircut in the first known work of literature, the *Epic of Gilgamesh*. At some point, then, people grew used to sitting down in the shade of some wide tree or by the warmth of the fire, breathing that little bit lighter as they felt the sharp blade moving close to their soft skin, talking or perhaps not talking, but trusting enough to know that they were safe, that they were being looked after.

And now, many thousands of years later, here I am, sitting in a metal chair in a quiet salon on a busy East London street, staring at my reflection in the mirror and waiting. Outside, people stroll along in the June sunshine, talking on their phones, music pouring out of the windows of passing cars, but in here the world feels remarkably still. The chair I'm sitting in is big and sturdy, all chrome and worn red leather and, with a cape fastened tightly around my neck, I feel ten years old again. I close my eyes and remember.

We would all ride the bus into town, my dad, my brother, and I, to go to Il Barbiere on Magdalene Street in Cambridge, where we would sit and wait our turn for a short back and sides, reading old magazines and bickering. I remember the wet, perfumy smell of the barbershop and how, when it was my turn, they would lay a stack of folded white towels on the chair to boost me up to the right height and how I would sit as still as I could, staring down at a framed picture of the boxer Rocky Marciano propped neatly on the sideboard, gloved fists held up to the camera.

In my present-day salon there are no framed pictures of boxing legends, only shelves full of expensive-looking haircare products, but the feeling is still the same. Propped up on my temporary throne, I am one part sun king, one part human sacrifice.

This is a familiar feeling but one I have not had for a while.

Whilst the pandemic smouldered away, all the hairdressers and barbershops in London were shut and people made do with self-administered trims or the best efforts of a flatmate or a loved one. Hair grew wild and free again. But now the world is reopening and for some reason I have made this trip to the hairdresser the first stop on my tentative journey back out into it. Why is that? Why begin here?

It is more than purely vanity. I have missed the experience of being in this salon. I have missed being sat here in this chair, swaddled in a cape, listening to the radio and the soft chirping of the scissors. I have missed the other less visible ways that a haircut prepares me for my entanglements with the social world. It is clear to me that I am not just here because my hair needs cutting, I am here for an encounter. I am here to experience a particular kind of care. A care that can be found nowhere else.

• • •

My hairdresser is called Susana. She is from Zaragoza in Spain. She has tattoos all the way up each thin arm and today is wearing a black vest top with the words *Daughters of Satan* written in big white letters. She is a pleasingly incongruous figure against the polite olive-green walls and designer tiles of the salon where she works.

Susana tells me that she always wanted to cut people's hair, that when she was little she used to cut all her dolls' hair, shorter and shorter and shorter until there was no more hair to cut, at which point she would run to her mum in tears. During lockdown, whilst her work as a hairdresser was temporarily suspended, she began rescuing sick and injured pigeons from the streets of London, bringing them to her small flat and slowly nursing them back to health. A year later she has created her own pigeon hospital and regularly receives calls from friends and rescue services about housing injured birds. She is currently looking after nine pigeons. She gives each of them a name when they arrive, all of them named for classical gods. Her most recent arrival is called Zeus.

According to Kurt Stenn in his book *Hair: A Human History*, some of the earliest hairdressers would have been medicine men, "spiritual caregivers" who made no distinction between treating the body and cutting hair. Their role was to balance the spirits of life and illness in the body, and to do so they would use "incantations, bloodletting, trepanning (boring holes into the skull), and hair removal to eliminate noxious spirits." These were mysterious and powerful figures in their communities, given responsibility for the bodies and the souls of those to whom they tended.

Susana may not look much like a medicine man or a witch doctor, but there is something quietly mystical about her. She wears that old magic lightly, but she wears it nonetheless. Susana has cut my hair for several years now. She is kind and friendly and talkative, but I am still also a little afraid of her.

It's not just Susana, though. I have always been a little afraid of hairdressers. It might be some lingering vestigial trace of their ancient, spiritual authority or it might be all those sharp scissors, but either way, in the chair I am in their power. There was the man at Il Barbiere in his plain white T-shirts with his picture of Rocky Marciano; the friend of my mum's who would come to our house seeming somehow more glamorous than anyone in our small village was entitled to be, like a visiting dignitary or an undercover Hollywood film star; there was Magda in Edinburgh, who ran a pop-up hairdresser's out of an anarchist café and offered each person who sat in her chair a shot of vodka; there was Richard at Open Barbers, who moved my parting from one side to the other in an act of unprecedented personal transformation; there was even, once, a nine-year-old boy who cut hair as part of a piece of performance art; and then there was Susana with her tattoos and her pigeons. I was in thrall to all of them.

Finding the right hairdresser is important. A 2018 survey by YouGov America found that over a third of Americans say they always get their hair cut by the same person, increasing to around half of those over the age of fifty-five, whilst a similar study in the UK found that over half of the women surveyed rated their relationship with their hairdresser as one of the ten most important relationships in their life.

When you find a good hairdresser you keep hold of them like few other things in your life. In their book *Hair Story*, Ayana Byrd and Lori Tharps tell the story of a man called Cecil Brown who spent thirty-one years looking for the perfect barber until he finally found him at a barbershop in Philadelphia. Now, on Saturdays, he gladly travels nearly an hour to the barbershop and then waits several hours more for his moment in the chair.

This commitment, this fervour, is about more than aesthetics. Of course people want a hairdresser who can cut their hair nicely, but they also want someone they can spend an hour or two or three in intimate proximity with. It is important that hairdressers know what they are doing when wielding sharp blades so close to our eyes and ears, and it is just as important that they know what to do with our secrets, our worries, our banal small talk, our weird opinions. We need to believe that they will use their old magic wisely. That when we are under their power, they will take care of us. A relationship with a hairdresser is a mystical, intangible thing. It is about chemistry, perhaps even a kind of alchemy. And when that alchemy works, you hold on to it.

• • •

I am sitting in my metal chair and Susana stands behind me, neither of us looking at each other directly. Instead, we are looking together at our own reflections in the giant salon mirror in front of us.

In *Encounters*, the sociologist Erving Goffman writes that an encounter is a "focused interaction" during which "people effectively agree to sustain for a time a single focus of cognitive and visual attention." According to Goffman, the effect of this shared and singular focus is to create a kind of temporary barrier between the people inside the encounter and everything happening outside of it. Stitched together in space and time, we create our own private reality, filtering out the parts of the world that are irrelevant to us and the encounter we are having. We become, for a while at least, a world unto ourselves.

Few encounters make this feel truer to me than a haircut. For this next hour or so, the entire world is contained in the mirror in front of me. All I can see is Susana and me. Neither of us really moves from this square metre or so of space. There are no phones. No screens. No intrusions from our lives outside of the salon. And our interaction is defined, for better or worse, by this profound, sometimes painful, lack of distraction. Yet, at the same time, this unbearable closeness is tempered by a kind of comforting distance. Making eye contact with Susana via her reflection in the mirror imbues our interaction with the illusion of a space between us that doesn't really exist, as if we were talking over the width of a coffee table rather than close enough to feel the warmth of each other's bodies on our skin.

Despite the density of modern cities, such intimacy with people who are not already close friends or lovers or members of our immediate family is unfamiliar and often uncomfortable. Our bodies react strangely to it. They prickle and flutter, clenching instinctively in anticipation of some more basic, physical human encounter; a confrontation of one kind or another.

The conventions of a haircut—the mirror, especially, but also the small talk, the cape, perhaps even a framed picture of a popular boxer—provide the means to help us navigate such closeness and the feelings it normally arouses. Inside this encounter, this miniature world, the awkwardness that normally accompanies bodies in intimate proximity is temporarily filtered out, and tenderness between relative strangers is accepted as normal.

But more even than this, looking in the mirror keeps Susana and me focused on the thing this encounter is really about—and that, unfortunately, is me. Although we are both visible in the frame, I am undoubtedly what Goffman might call "the single focus of cognitive and visual attention." There I am, sitting right at the centre of the picture. A head on display, preparing to spend the next hour looking at myself as penance for the apparent vanity of wanting to get a haircut in the first place.

To see myself and to recognise myself being seen by others in this way is a part of learning to be human. Our whole sense of self is bound up in our relationship to the mirror. We use it to identify the moment at which babies become self-aware, and, more questionably, to differentiate animals that have self-recognition from those that don't. It is shorthand for our capacity to recognise ourselves as individuals bound up in a fluid and dynamic relationship with the world around us. An encounter that is navigated via a giant mirror cannot help but be about the way we see ourselves, and our desire to understand the way other people see us.

In this way, the mirror that confronts us in the barbershop or the salon is not only there to show us our haircut in progress, but to act as a reminder of why our hair matters so much to us in the first place. It is a reminder of all the ways in which we are constantly caught in the twin acts of self-recognition and self-presentation, preparing a face to meet the faces that we meet.

• • •

It is at this point, the two of us stood there together in the mirror, that Susana always asks the same question, offered up each time like the opening line of a song we both know all the words to: *What can I do for you today?*

As she says it the world stops, the ceiling fans cease circling, the hairdryer cuts out, the radio falls silent, every car on the street comes to an immediate halt, birds are suspended in the air like ornaments hanging in a shop window. The sole living thing in an otherwise unmoving world, I stare at my reflection in the mirror and consider this question's two possible answers.

Somewhere deep in my chest I hear the low gurgle of the answer I want to give.

What I want to tell her is to go wild. To do something completely new. Something outrageous. To shave it all off, or half of it off, or bleach it or dye it like a colour wheel. I want her to make it look like George Michael in the '80s or Winona Ryder in the '90s or like an extra from a film about outlaws escaping from a prison ship in outer space. I want her to be adventurous. I want her to be bold. *I* want to be bold. I want to be braver than I really am. I want the moment where I look up into the mirror and hardly recognise the person staring back at me. I want, more than anything, to be transformed.

They promised us a haircut could do this. Right from the beginning we were sold this particular dream. It is as old as our written record of haircutting itself. It is this idea of what a haircut can be that features in the ancient Mesopotamian poem the *Epic of Gilgamesh*, written on a series of stone tablets over three thousand years ago.

The *Epic of Gilgamesh* tells the story of the ancient Sumerian king Gilgamesh and a wild man called Enkidu, sent by the gods to stop the king from oppressing his people. Enkidu is raw nature incarnate, pre-human, as much beast as man, born from all the dirt and freedom and disorder of the world. Frightened of his primitive power, Gilgamesh sends the sacred prostitute Shamhat to seduce Enkidu, which she does remarkably successfully. After a week of relentless lovemaking Shamhat leads Enkidu to a green meadow where he drinks seven goblets of wine, causing his spirit to loosen and his face to shine. At which point a barber arrives and he has a haircut. With all the vestiges of his former wildness sheared away, Enkidu is transformed. He becomes a Man, a citizen of the modern world; separated forever from his animal spirit, he is now fit to walk the streets of the great metropolis of Uruk, fit even to become the most intimate companion of the king himself.

Here then begins our very human love affair with the myth of the transformative makeover. It is a story which has persisted across millennia, becoming the staple of Hollywood romcoms, from *Cinderella* to *Sabrina* to *She's All That*, and the conceit behind approximately a billion hours of reality television. Because who doesn't love an epic makeover? Who is not thrilled by that moment when the chair spins or the dry ice parts or the camera pans back to reveal a completely new person standing there before you, carved from the rough marble of the old one? And when we see that new person, how we all scream or cry or hold our hands to our mouths in shock and wonder. It is a kind of magic.

On YouTube you can find a whole subgenre of video in which barbers and hairdressers in various parts of the world film themselves giving a free haircut to a member of their local homeless population. It is a problematic, exploitative, and utterly compelling piece of self-promotion. In my favourite video we are introduced to Jose Antonio, known as "The Spirit of the Square," in the sleepy corner of Mallorca that he calls his home. At the beginning of the film he looks wiry and ancient, as wild as Enkidu, his white hair cascading out from under an old baseball cap to meet the ends of his straggly white beard. He tells us that he is trying to get his life together, that he parks cars to save up enough money for a room to live in. We watch as the hairdresser carefully begins trimming and shaving, massaging shampoo into his scalp and applying dye to his hair and beard.

After she has finished he looks not like a new version of himself, but rather a different man entirely: a charismatic middle-aged lounge singer or the author of a series of popular science fiction novels or a long-lost son in search of the father he never knew or the ghost of Christmases past, here to remind the real Jose Antonio of what once was and could be again. "You're not Jose Antonio," he says tearfully to his reflection. "No one will recognise me . . . as long as I don't tell them who I am, no one will recognise me . . . this has totally changed me. It's not me."

And when he walks back into the square in his new dark sunglasses, we believe in this transformation. We believe that something deeper, more profound than his hair has changed. We believe, even if only for a few seconds, that remaking oneself is that easy. That magic is real.

This, in the end, is what I want to believe, not just for Jose Antonio but also for me, for all of us. I want to believe that there is hope for us, too, that we might be just as easily reborn, might yet become the people we want to be. I want to believe in the possibility of our collective redemption. From Enkidu onwards, the implication has always been clear: a haircut has a sacred power that goes beyond appearances. It is a reshaping of the body that works its way deep into the soul.

I still dream of just such a metamorphosis, believing there might be some newer, better version of myself buried under my current hairstyle. When I'm facing the mirror and Susana asks me what I want doing, this is what I want to tell her. I want to tell her to take her scissors and cut me open, to reach down inside and find the new me hidden in there. But I never do.

The closest I ever got to summoning the necessary bravery was when I was seventeen years old and my mum's glamorous hairdresser friend agreed to dye my hair red. I had just started sixth form (junior year in the US) after five gruellingly lonely and miserable years of secondary school. I was ready to meet new friends, to become a new person. I remember the chemical smell of the dye as I sat on an uncomfortable dining room chair in the middle of the kitchen floor. And I remember the thrill of it, the lightness in my chest, how close the alchemy of reinvention briefly felt. But even then I had opted only for some semi-permanent option that never made it as far as red, giving up at a deep orange and fading quickly to an anaemic pink. I hid my new hair under a baseball cap for several days until the dye had been washed away completely.

It is no surprise to me that I am not the adventurer I would like to be, but it is always something of a disappointment. I am still too attached to the old version of myself, too afraid that I might not like the new one.

And so when the world begins moving again, when the fan starts circling and the radio crackles back to life, I always give the second answer. I tell Susana that I would like the same as last time, that I want my hair to continue to look roughly as it did before. Maybe a bit shorter or longer at the front. Maybe with the clippers on the sides rather than the scissors. But fundamentally it should be the same. I am asking her to maintain the person I already am.

This answer is exactly what Susana has been expecting. She smiles and agrees, and then she guides me to the sinks at the back of the salon and begins washing my hair.

• • •

The first time a hairdresser washed my hair, I thought she might be playing some kind of trick on me. I was twenty years old, in a proper hairdresser's rather than a barbershop for possibly the first time. The hairdresser left me at the back of the room with a hot towel over my face, and all I could think was that everyone else in the salon, customers and staff alike, was looking over and laughing. Such care, some people might dismissively call it pampering, was uncomfortable to me because I was so unused to it. I was used to having my hair cut in a room where Rocky Marciano was always there to reassure me that nothing unmanly was about to take place.

Now I think nothing of the fact that Susana finishes washing my hair by massaging my head, the tips of her fingers moving in small circles across my skull. How I love this part now, this pampering, this little anachronism, this gentle vestige of a time when the person who cut your hair might also treat the rest of your ailments, lance your boils, bleed you if you needed it.

Throughout history and across cultures, haircutting has been a service that people at all levels of society could access, which meant that for many people the care you received there was often the only kind of care available to you outside of your immediate family.

The link between hairdressers and surgery goes back nearly a thousand years. In 1215 the Roman Catholic Church decreed that it was inappropriate for monks to perform any kind of surgery, and so across Europe their knowledge and their tools were transferred to local barbers, who were considered the most suitable people for this new role given their familiarity with razor blades and scissors. For the following five hundred years, in Europe at least, most of the medical treatments available to ordinary people were performed by barbers. At a time when learned medical professionals were limited to courts and universities, they provided the closest thing most ordinary people could get to regular medical care. In China, too, traditional street barbers performed essential medical procedures, travelling from town to town, ringing a bell to announce their arrival.

The most obvious reminder of barbering's past association with surgery is the red, white, and occasionally blue pole outside many traditional barbershops (including Il Barbiere in Cambridge). The colours on the pole signify the blood and bandages involved in bloodletting, whilst the pole itself is a symbolic representation of an actual bloodied and bandaged pole that patients would grip onto whilst the bloodletting took place, and which would then be left outside the shop as a bracingly graphic demonstration of the kind of services offered inside. Like the laminated pictures of brightly coloured breakfasts in the windows of a café, but in every way worse.

Whilst this gruesome little advertisement may be the most visible connection between hairdressing and medicine, the relationship continues to persist in other ways as well, not least in the way hairdressers of various kinds think about themselves and their job. It is there in the head rubs and the hot towels, in the free cups of tea and the agony aunt chats, in a barber's commitment to the antiquated art of the cut-throat razor. As Nat "The Bush Doctor" Mathis, hairdresser extraordinaire and self-proclaimed inventor of the Afro, once said, "I'm just doctoring the hair. I'm a doctor."

Online I found an interview with the great Bush Doctor himself, filmed in his little basement hair salon in Capitol Heights, Maryland. In it he talks softly about his life as a hairdresser—how he got his nickname, his many hairdressing inventions, how he came to meet and cut hair for the funk musician Chuck Brown, his love of singing, his former life as a roller-skating instructor. The camera scans across the room, picking out details from the salon, the detritus of a life well lived: neatly framed newspaper clippings, a photograph of Nat and Chuck grinning under a street sign for Chuck Brown Way, a painting of Nat as a handsome young man in a powder-grey suit, a sign reading, "Let Your Hair Be My Problem."

"I remember one time I was thinking of getting out of the business," Nat says, "and one person told me, they said, 'You can't get out of the business, you have too many people's images that you have to care for.'" And when he says this, about the images he cares for, I want to be there, amidst that clutter of knick-knacks and mementos, breathing in the damp air, listening to the music of scissors and clippers.

Hairdressers are a particular kind of caregiver, whose roots run much deeper into the lives of ordinary people than any modern medical professional. And we might think of our encounters with them as acts of caregiving. From the moment when you settle into a familiar chair in front of a familiar mirror in a salon or barbershop or at home in the middle of the kitchen, you are being cared for.

A hairdresser takes care. Care both in the sense that they recognise and appreciate all the very real, very human meanings that our hair holds for us, and in the sense that they approach us with a certain precision, with calmness, with deliberate, methodical grace. And as has always been the case, hairdressers are for the majority of ordinary people the most common and consistent caregiver outside of their immediate family. A source of respite, remedy, and repair on almost any high street anywhere in the world.

In the UK alone there are around 41,000 hair and beauty businesses employing around 287,000 people, about the same as the number of nurses in the country and more than twice the number of opticians, physiotherapists, psychiatrists, and dentists put together. Barbershops and hair salons continue to rank amongst the ten most popular new businesses, which is perhaps unsurprising when you consider that on average, men and women in the UK visit a hairdresser approximately every six weeks, or eight times a year.

When the coronavirus pandemic shut down the world, there was much joking about the impact it had upon our hair. On Zoom screens across the world people began transforming like slow-motion werewolves, Enkidus in reverse, their hair breaking free of the styling that had contained it, growing wild and untamed, like weeds overtaking a neglected garden. Roots showing, ends split, beards everywhere. People commiserated with each other and waited impatiently for the salons to open again, which eventually they did.

And when they did we celebrated; we admired our reclaimed style, our highlights, our fringes, our flat-top fades, these little pieces of ourselves we had back again. But did we think enough about the other, less tangible things we had reclaimed? Did you appreciate your reacquaintance with that old soothing magic? With that ancient variety of careful attention? Did you feel that familiar warmth again, those hands moving over and around you, the comfort of being held in this very particular way?

• • •

I am back in the chair again. Susana is teasing my wet hair into the recovery position and I am waiting with bated breath for that first snip to happen. That moment when the scissors slice shut. The soft metallic cough as metal kisses metal and a first few curls of wet hair fall gently onto my shoulder. It is not a big deal, and yet maybe it also is.

Arguably the most famous of all haircuts is described in the Old Testament story of Samson and Delilah. Samson was a warrior blessed by God with outlandish strength who once massacred an entire Philistine army using only the jawbone of a donkey. He was a Nazirite, which meant he had made a vow to God which included the promise never to cut his hair. When he revealed this to his lover, Delilah, she betrayed him to the

Philistines. "And she made him sleep upon her knees; and she called for a man, and had the seven locks of his head shaven off; and she began to afflict him, and his strength went from him." (Judges 16:19)

The story of Samson and Delilah is told as a kind of warning, like so many other tedious warnings that men have issued through history, about the dangers of trusting the wrong woman. But what remains interesting about it is the way it imbues something as ordinary and domestic as a haircut with such tragic gravity. In Rubens's famous painting of the scene, Samson lies face down in Delilah's lap, his naked back as vast as a continent, a landscape of muscle and bone glowing amber in the flickering candlelight. A bearded servant leans over him, hands gently twisting as he reaches out to cut the first lock of hair, whilst Delilah watches on and soldiers gather in the doorway. Everything in the painting turns around this action, the scissor blades poised to close on a thick brown ringlet. It is the eye at the centre of Rubens's baroque storm of colour and light. The explosion at the beginning of the universe. Every grain of paint on the canvas holds its breath, waiting for those scissors to close. This is a haircut elevated to the status of cataclysm. The snip heard around the world.

I may not feel like my hair is touched by God, but I still feel that tingle of transgression when the scissors first close around it. As I await that first snip I can feel an illicit thrill, like ancient sorcery. Try picking up a pair of scissors now and cutting off even a few thin strands. To me, it still feels dangerous. A spell of transformation that hovers briefly in the air and then is gone just as quickly.

Do other people feel this? In lockdown, as people began lifting pairs of scissors tentatively towards their own heads or those of their friends or relatives, did they feel that slight shake in their hand, that flicker of doubt, that crackle on their tongue, the metallic tang of some centuries-old promise being broken?

Or does the anxiety of those first few snips have another, more modern cause? In the pre-capitalist world, most hairdressers might have been medicine men, community elders or servants, their work intimately connected to a very specific set of cultural or religious practices, but now they are businesspeople as well as caregivers, and hairdressing in the present age is another product in a marketplace. As such, your style of haircut is as much about individual choice and private desire as it is about collective tradition.

This inevitably leads to the issue of communication. How do you go about explaining to your hairdresser what it is you want? How many magazine pictures are enough? Whenever I have attempted to ask for anything even vaguely new, I have watched my haircut take shape whilst gripped by a very particular kind of angst: a silent, internal howl. How is it going? Does that look good? Will they get it right? If it starts to go wrong, will I have the courage to say I don't like it?

This failure to communicate, the problem of a breakdown in trust or understanding, is surely the great dread of any contemporary haircutting experience. In the '90s TV sitcom *Friends*, for example, in an episode where Phoebe reluctantly agrees to cut Monica's hair, Phoebe confuses Dudley Moore with Demi Moore, leaving Monica not with the stylish pixie cut of a young Hollywood sex symbol, but rather the neat, square mullet of a middle-aged British comedian. You may never have experienced a haircutting disaster quite this bad, but surely most people have felt some equivalent to Monica's guttural horror when she realises Phoebe's mistake, her hands reaching instinctively up to her head, grasping at the ends of her ruined hair as if she's trying to stem the bleeding.

• • •

Despite the fear associated with that initial cut, I quickly relax into things. Susana's salon is a safe place to me. It is somewhere I enjoy coming to, where the time seems to pass all too quickly.

Salons are rooms suffused by care, and as such an important kind of refuge from the rest of the world. For many people, the care they receive here is one of the most important and consistent forms of care they experience in their lives. It is a care that is manifested in many different ways, as learning, as friendship, as community.

David L. Shabazz describes Black barbershops in the US as "discursive spaces where identity is shaped as young men are initiated into manhood and African American culture." Here the haircut is the magnet holding together a larger social ecosystem. Men come to have their hair cut, but also to hang out, to watch sports or the news, to listen to music, and, most importantly, to talk.

Steve James's epic documentary portrait of Chicago and its people, *City So Real*, begins and ends with the city's barbershops. They are his portal into the everyday life of the city. There is, on the one hand, the barbershop full of retired white police officers at Joe's on 26th Street, the walls mosaiced with pictures of the Chicago Cubs and Tiger Woods, where they gather to eat dense slices of rich apple strudel, tease each other relentlessly, and complain that things aren't how they used to be. And then, elsewhere on the South Side, there is Sideline Studio on a street split by a commuter rail line, its only signage a canvas banner pinned above the glass door. Inside, the young Black barber works away with his clippers and argues animatedly with an older man waiting for his turn in the chair. Their argument, like so many arguments in so many places, is about young people today, and what older people think is wrong with them and what younger people think those older people don't understand. The argument flows back and forth, voices rising, other clients joining in. It is hard at points because the disagreement itself is hard, even intractable. But in the end we see the older man take his place in the chair, and the young barber with his clippers, gently shaping and reshaping.

And there is something to be witnessed here, about the kind of tenderness that a haircut demands, about how that gentleness permeates the room, how it insinuates itself into the conversations that are had there. "I say this because I love you," the young barber says at the argument's most strained point, and there *is* love here. A love that exists outside of the bonds of family, across ideologies and profound divisions of opinion. A love that is essential and increasingly rare.

The same kind of love can be seen at Open Barbers in London, the UK's first queer- and trans-friendly hair salon. Open Barbers was founded in 2011 as a twice-a-month pop-up in a tiny hair salon in Kennington by two trans men, Greygory Vass and Felix Lane. They were inspired to do so by their own fraught and often humiliating experiences of getting haircuts, where judgements about gender were frequent even in supposedly unisex salons. With Open Barbers they wanted to create a space that was open to a broader, more expansive understanding of gender and identity and the part that our hair has in determining both how the world sees us and how we think about ourselves. Such was the demand for the kind of environment Greygory and Felix provided that within a few years they had opened their own permanent salon with an ever-expanding team of stylists.

More than anything, Open Barbers is about belonging. From their fire-engine-red shop just by Shoreditch Park, Greygory, Felix, and their team aim to give anyone who wants or needs it the kind of caring encounter that more conventional hairdressers and barbers have long provided for cis-gendered people. And perhaps inevitably, for that reason the shop has become far more than just a place to get your hair cut. It is a place where people come for acupuncture and massage, for therapy, for community-related gatherings, or simply to hang out, read books, study, sit and let time pass in a place of safety.

It is a place where queer people can come to feel comfort-

able and cared for at a time when assaults on the trans community are as frequent and violent as they have ever been. As Felix
recently told *Diva* magazine, "We hold space for people on days
that might be important for queer related reasons. They don't
necessarily have to talk about it or declare it, but you can be here
and we'll acknowledge and hold that space for you."

Just as a haircut is more than the simple act of cutting hair,
and a hairdresser is more than someone that cuts that hair, so
too a barbershop or a salon is, for so many people, a more important part of their life than its basic function might suggest. There
is no other space quite like it. It is a place of community and
belonging. A space of tenderness. A soft place in an often-hard
world. A place of continuity at a time of relentless and exhausting change.

In a world of increasing automation and atomisation, when
so many of our encounters are mediated by computers and the
internet, there is something incredibly comforting for a lot of
people about the fact that the basic process of having our hair
cut has changed so little over time. That we still sit now, in the
shade maybe or by the warmth of a fire, feeling the sharp blade
moving close to our soft skin, talking or perhaps not talking,
but trusting enough to know that we are safe, that we are being
looked after.

● ● ●

Susana's scissors are stuttering their way around my head now,
the shorn hair collecting in the folds of my cape like mountain

snow. As she works she gently tilts my head into the position she requires, like she's rearranging flowers in a vase. With the rest of my body concealed under a long black cape I am nothing but a bobbing head, tilting obediently one way and then another.

There are very few situations in which I so freely give up my bodily autonomy. As we grow up, most of us are taught, quite reasonably and rightly, that our bodies are our own. The politics of who is allowed to touch us, to manipulate us, is fraught and complex and has only grown more so over time. To manipulate once meant simply to skilfully handle objects (such as a human head, perhaps), but since the nineteenth century it has also, in relation to people, taken on a more negative meaning: to covertly influence or exploit. Are we now more prone to see bad intentions in any attempt to manipulate us, physically or otherwise? As we have grown more cognisant of the historic abuses of people's bodily autonomy, the visible and invisible violence that scars our relationships to one another, have we become less trusting of the way people touch us, move us, manipulate us?

A good hairdresser, a hairdresser we trust, is one of the few people in the world we allow to manipulate us. We trust their good intentions, their training, their character. Perhaps we even see in them the residue of those centuries-old practices of caregiving and healing. And having this space, where we are safely touched and moved and repositioned, is good, healthy even. Physical touch has been linked to lower blood pressure, higher oxytocin levels, and better sleep. But more than this, giving yourself up to somebody else's authority for a while, allowing your whole body to be under their control, demands a kind of trust that in today's world feels radical. Such trust, written deep into the flesh and bone of our bodies, is a valuable kind of refuge from the suspicion, cynicism, and outright fakery that defines so many of our encounters with each other in the digital space, where manipulation through spam emails, "fake news," and social media grifters is never more than a click or two away.

The most memorable haircut I have ever had was ten years ago, on a warm July afternoon in a small salon just off Hoxton Square, as part of a project called Haircuts by Children by the Toronto-based theatre company Mammalian Diving Reflex. The company works with a group of local children who are trained by a hairstylist in the essentials of haircutting—how to use the scissors and clippers, how to dye, even how to attempt to cut patterns into the client's hair. They then take over a local salon for a weekend, cutting the hair of willing clients who book for the experience in the same way you might book a ticket to the theatre.

As I walked towards the salon through the lazy afternoon sunshine, I had already formed a clear picture in my mind of what kind of encounter this would be. I braced myself for what I condescendingly imagined would be a kind of ritual punishment, a frantic, chaotic hairmageddon of careless scissors slashing into my hair like a helicopter accident. A manifestation of the kind of relentless, chaotic anarchy that so many adults assume is the texture of everyday childhood life, having forgotten the quiet seriousness that is an equally important part of being young.

In reality my hairdresser sat me down in that familiar over-sized chair, we stared at each other in the mirror, and he asked me what I would like done with all the thoughtfulness of someone who cared deeply about doing a good job. Someone who wanted to take care of me. At which point it occurred to me that I had arrived at this encounter completely lacking in trust. Trust that he would do a good job, but trust also that someone so young could ever look after me, could ever be responsible for me. Looking back now, it seems to me that Haircuts by Children wasn't really about haircutting at all; it was about who we allow ourselves to trust, and the power we imbue them with by doing so.

Within the few brief minutes it took him to organise his clippers and decide upon the style he thought was best, I was back in that state of quiet suspension that a good haircut always leads me to. That place of absolute trust. Suddenly, I was nine years old again, on my stack of towels at Il Barbiere, listening to the radio and moving my head obediently forward and back.

● ● ●

I can sense with a certain amount of disappointment that my haircut is nearly over. Susana is neatening up the sides with a slim pair of clippers; I can feel their insistent buzz running gently around my ear. The salon is nearly empty. There is just one other woman allowing her dye to settle on the other side of the room. Susana brushes stray hairs from my neck, unclips me from my cape and whisks it away, like the reveal at the end of a magic trick.

In truth, if this is a magic trick, it is somewhat underwhelming. The new me looks pretty much the same as the old me. No mystical transformation has taken place. No romcom glow-up. I am just a little neater round the edges. For me the magic is not this moment at the end, it is the hour that preceded it. That care that feels like a gift and the trust I can offer in return. By the end, something important has been reset. The fraying of my connection to the world soothed and conditioned.

I step outside, and on the street the world feels ever so slightly charged, everything infused with the glow of that soft salon light.

CHAPTER 2

SIX SMALL INTERRUPTIONS

1. The Lady in the Yellow Coat

It is an unremarkable Tuesday morning and on a little street beside a river in a quiet English town an encounter between two strangers is about to occur.

If this were a film we might freeze the action for a moment here to better enable you to take it all in—me, wrapped in my winter coat, standing in front of an older lady dressed in bright yellow, my arms open, hers deep in her pockets. I'm wearing my friendliest face, but nonetheless she is looking at me in confusion, unsure why she has been stopped, who I am, or what it is that I want from her. There might be a flicker of annoyance haunting the corners of her eyes, or it could just be my imagination. Around us the world floats on in its quiet Tuesday morning way. Students rushing to class at the nearby community college. An older man taking a quiet constitutional. Two nursery leaders pushing a small platoon of toddlers in a pair of bright red trolleys. Swans drifting in lazy circles on the river. The sky a steely January blue.

I am in Bedford, conducting TV interviews with random

members of the public as part of a project my partner, Beckie, and I are making with a group of local primary school children. We are taking it in turns to approach people and ask them if they would like to be interviewed, but every time my turn comes around, something inside me resists. I see the stranger approaching, but cannot will myself to speak to them. My body recoils from the encounter. I feel as if I am stood on the lip of a diving board, willing myself to leap into the water below but feeling a sudden heaviness in chest and in my legs as my body drags itself back towards the safety of solid ground.

The thing I am feeling is a kind of dread. That animal fear that lives deep in our bones. Something about the idea of speaking with this nice lady in the yellow coat is filling me with a primal sense of foreboding. It's not that I am afraid of her, but I am afraid of *this*—this potential interaction, this *encounter*. Something about it feels undeniably dreadful to me.

I don't think I am the only one who feels this way. In 2014, when an anonymous group started handing out little blue pin badges on the London Underground inviting people to chat to each other, locals reacted with horror, describing the idea as a "monstrosity," "a living hell," and, perhaps not entirely seriously, as an attempt to "undermine the fabric of society." Why is this? What is it about the prospect of speaking with strangers that we find so viscerally uncomfortable? So absolutely dreadful?

The obvious answer is that most of us are profoundly out of practice at it. Indeed, according to the University of Chicago psychologist Juliana Schroeder, we speak to strangers so rarely that we have begun to forget that when we do, we usually enjoy it. Schroeder and her colleague Nicholas Epley created a series of experiments involving participants striking up conversations with strangers on their daily commute. From these studies Schroeder and Epley discovered that the *idea* of talking with a stranger was predicted by participants to be a negative experience when, in reality, it was an almost overwhelmingly positive one.

The primary reason people gave for assuming the worst of this prospective interaction was that they thought the stranger would have no interest in talking with them. They worried that because of this, their overture would be rejected. Most of us seem to have so fully absorbed the idea that people don't enjoy talking to one another that we fear that all these people we are sharing the street with want nothing to do with us. We fear that, should we dare approach them, whatever our justification for doing so, they will look at us with nothing but horror and scorn. We fear rejection and this has, over time, metastasised into dread, which only helps reinforce the tendency to avoid one another.

It wasn't always like this. In England, for example, in the Middle Ages, the streets of a market town like Bedford would have been the busy centre of public life. Living quarters, shops, and workshops would open out on to streets thronged with people, where hawkers and craftspeople would sell their wares. In these transgressive, polyphonous spaces, public and private were slurred together in the tumult and the mud, and encounters with

31

all kinds of people were unavoidable—minstrels, apothecaries, butchers, con men, criminals, drunkards, surgeons, travelling salespeople, and local aristocracy.

Successive waves of social and technological change in the centuries since then—the Industrial Revolution, separate spheres, the rise of the suburbs—have transformed our relationship to the streets we walk on and our expectations of the kinds of encounters we will have there. Today, we live and work very differently. Factories, warehouses, and offices are all private, interior spaces dedicated exclusively to work and open only to the people who work there. People's homes tend to be on residential streets or in residential buildings with little day-to-day street life beyond an occasional polite hello to a neighbour. Mass transportation systems like metros and buses—and, more significantly, the all-pervading dominance of the car—have radically transformed how people use the streets of our towns and cities, foregrounding their role as transit routes and drastically reducing the space people have to meet and mingle.

In turn our shopping and socialising habits have also changed, away from congregating in urban centres and towards more stratified and segregated destinations. COVID-19 has only accelerated this process through the requirement to work, shop, and socialise from home. The shops that once brought people to the town centre are closing down or already boarded up, the public drawn away, first by out-of-town shopping centres and retail parks, and then by the allure of not having to leave the house at all. All these changes have helped create a much more definitive separation between the private spaces in which we predominantly live and work and our increasingly diminished public realm.

This goes some way towards explaining why I might be so out of practice at speaking with strangers. It is something that we no longer expect to do when we are out walking in urban space. Most modern streets are no longer swarmed by hawkers and tradespeople. Instead they are designed primarily as spaces of transit. Stood on our Bedford street, our camcorder mounted on its tripod and our little pile of rucksacks marking our temporary occupation of this spot, we are the exception to the norm. The only people standing still whilst everyone else is moving, flowing swiftly past us on their way to somewhere else.

On streets where people do little else than walk, it is much harder to approach a stranger. When we walk we tend not to leave much, if any, space for interactions with the people around us. Think, for example, about that most famous category of urban walker, the flaneur, whose most important quality is their sense of detachment. The flaneur is a solitary observer, experiencing the material conditions of the city and its people as a private phantasmagoria. They move through the city as if in a dream. Such walking takes us away from where we are, literally and figuratively, separating us from the strangers around us who are themselves contained within the movement of their own interior trajectories.

Here we all are, then, together and not together, making our own way through streets that are at once more crowded and emptier than they have ever been. Moving from one place to another, each of us assuming that the people around us want nothing to do with us. I am separated from the people around me by a canyon of unknowing. Or at least, this is the way I make sense of the wings beating in my chest and the tightening in my throat as I prepare to explain myself to the elderly lady in the yellow coat. This feeling of weightlessness, my body falling through the air as I smile, make eye contact, and open my mouth to speak.

2. A Teenage Couple on Hudson Street

The photograph is black and white, and in it a couple stand together in front of a bare brick wall. The first thing I notice is their faces. First hers, then his. Their hair is neat and dark and their expressions are, to me, unreadable. His eyes dart leftwards but hers look straight down the barrel of the camera. They are *so young*. That is the thing that strikes me most. Baby-faced, standing there on Hudson Street in their adult coats and smart shoes. He stands on the left, one arm wrapped tenderly around her, his fingers gripping her coat at the shoulder, and the other shoved deep into his pocket. Her patterned dress and his shirt and tie. I don't even know their names. They are just two young people who happened to be in the right place at the right time one day in 1963 to have their portrait taken by Diane Arbus.

Teenage Couple on Hudson Street, N.Y.C. 1963 is one of a series of photographs of young couples in the city that Arbus began to take around this time. She was forty years old and had been separated from her husband and collaborator, Allan Arbus, for four years. She was entering what was arguably her creative peak as a photographer, the feverish period when many of her most iconic photographs were taken. When she wasn't on a paid shoot or looking after her two daughters, she roamed the city, spending hours of the day and night compulsively seeking out people to photograph. One day she might be drifting through Central Park, approaching families or children, playing the role of the sweet, ditzy amateur photographer simply capturing snaps for her collection. The next she could be ducking in and out of clubs and bars, taking dressing-room portraits of strippers and drag queens, or heading out to New Jersey to find burlesque shows and nudist beaches, sometimes even venturing as far as Pennsylvania in pursuit of people living and working on the margins of society at the cheap and grotty circuses known as "mud shows"—magicians, bearded ladies, dwarves—the kind of people her photographs return to again and again, to honour or exploit, depending on who you believe. Failing all of this, she could be found closer to her home in Manhattan, in the working-class neighbourhoods around the Hudson River piers, amongst a differently marginalised set of people, lingering on street corners in the hope of finding someone, anyone, whose life and face compelled her.

Only a year before this photograph was taken Arbus had switched from shooting with a thirty-five millimetre Nikon camera to a twin-lens Rolleiflex. The shift was important. Whereas the former was lightweight and easy to hold, capturing the kind of grainy street photography that describes the world in a blur of movement, the Rolleiflex was bulkier and more difficult to handle but produced images of clarity and sharpness, enabling her, in her own words, "to see the real difference between things."

But more than just transforming the texture of her photography, this change of equipment also required a profound transformation in Arbus's relationship to her subjects. Rather than lifting the camera to her face and quickly focusing, as she had previously been able to do, she needed to hold the Rolleiflex at waist level, with the image then carefully adjusted by looking down into the camera, a technique complicated enough that she initially feared she wouldn't be able to master it. No longer able to move so discreetly, flaneur-like, through the whirl of the busy city, Arbus now operated in moments of suspension and interruption. She stood face to face with the strangers in front of her, smiling and talking with them whilst she prepped the camera, able to look them straight in the eye as the picture was taken. Street photography reimagined as an act of encounter.

For the naturally shy and quiet Arbus, this meant everything. She used this camera as an invitation and occasionally a crowbar, a means of levering her way into lives of people radically different to herself. Here was a woman who grew up in comfort and relative solitude, now scrabbling to reach outwards into a world from which her parents' money had insulated her. Walking the streets in search of experiences, encounters, connections. She loved these interactions, describing them to her long-time confidante Marvin Israel as "adventures." "The photograph was like her trophy—it was what she received as an award for her adventure," he would later say.

What is *Teenage Couple on Hudson Street, N.Y.C. 1963* really a photograph of, then? In part it is a portrait of the two young people in the centre of the frame, but it is also a document of a moment. A photograph of an encounter. It is an image haunted by the invisible presence of the photographer herself, her life and its many fractured parts. And when thought of in this way it is, more than anything, a photograph of difference. A portrait of the many things that separate one side of the camera from the other—age, wealth, religion, an understanding of the world and one's place within it. When you look at their expressions—uncomfortable, curious, maybe a little annoyed, a little amused—you can see that difference hanging in the monochrome air, captured as sharply and as clearly as the figures in the photograph themselves.

The word *encounter* comes from the late Latin *in contra*, meaning to be "in front of," and was originally used to mean a meeting of adversaries or a confrontation. The person you encountered was once always a foe or an opponent. Still today we talk of encountering difficulties and encountering problems, recognising that an encounter will always be an interruption in the trajectory of our own desires. A meeting with a world outside of ourselves.

Buried in the history of the word is the notion of difference. To encounter someone is to recognise them as a person separate to you, with separate thoughts, experiences, and opinions. To think of our meetings with others as encounters is to highlight that when two or more people meet, difference is always present and the meeting is in some ways an attempt to navigate that difference. These everyday encounters are the places where our lives rub up against the lives of the people living around us, both people we know and people we don't; those who are similar to us and those who are not.

Cities are and always have been crucibles of difference. Difference is their keynote. Their repeated refrain. They are places of wealth and poverty, centres of power and sites of marginalisation and destitution. Places where capitalism draws breath, pulling all manner of people towards itself and leaving them there to jostle for space and opportunity. To some extent, all these people exist within different realms of the city. There are corporate districts and industrial quarters, affluent suburbs and subsidised housing schemes. Places of explicit and implicit exclusion. But these differentiated zones are never absolute and the boundaries between them never unbreachable. In a city, you are usually surrounded by people very different to yourself. Despite the fact that we spend so little time there, the streets remain the places where we are most intimately proximate with strangers and their otherness. We wait at the same traffic lights, queue for the same buses. Fumble past each other on the same narrow pavements. As we navigate these streets we are also implicitly navigating the differences between us. Describing the inequities and the complexities of our societies through an improvised choreography of living bodies and their sometimes-fraught encounters with one another.

These interactions are sites of friction and possibility, of anxiety and joy. There is a spontaneity to an encounter that demands we approach it with a degree of uncertainty and vulnerability, a softness that leaves space for compassion and empathy in a world where both can often be in short supply. An encounter is an opportunity. It can thread cracks through our perception of the world, allowing for the possibility that new light might come spilling in. What do we lose when we stop inhabiting the streets of our towns and cities? What understanding of the world, and of each other, are we depriving ourselves of as we spend less and less time in proximity to all these strangers and their lives that are so very different from our own?

Diane Arbus's photographs are uncompromising and unsentimental. They have sharp edges. They are difficult photographs because the encounters they document were also often difficult. They acknowledge the unbridgeable separation between her and her subjects. "It's impossible to get out of your skin and into somebody else's," she once said. "Somebody else's tragedy is not the same as your own."

3. The Man Outside the Supermarket

The man outside the supermarket and I used to speak maybe once or twice a week, but recently I feel like I am always letting him down. We used to say hello, and if I had any change I would give it to him happily. We would share a fist bump and comment on the weather, him leaning on the silver rail by the shopping carts, me locking up my bike next to him. Our interactions were always friendly, familiar, but freighted with all that remained unspoken. Privileges and inequities. All that discomforting difference. We must have asked each other how we are doing more than a hundred times, but I have never asked his name. And yet I looked forward to seeing him there, and I hope he thought the same.

I don't tend to have many other encounters like this in London. They have been designed out of my journeys through the city, allowing me to move with frictionless ease from one place to another. Partly this is something that has been done for me by architects and urban planners whose zeal to fill the city with space and light and order often results in urban environments expunged of discomfort and uncertainty. Polite modernist piazzas with sunken fountains and tasteful public art, quietly patrolled by private security staff. Hostile architecture like tactically positioned spikes in otherwise comfortable resting places and benches with sloping designs that aggressively discourage rough sleeping or even groups of people who might want to gather for extended lengths of time. Retail parks and out-of-town shopping arcades take car-driving members of the public away from the city centres and out to areas that are reserved solely for them and other car users.

All of this is about control—controlling the way people move through the city, controlling the encounters they might have there. And though in theory I resent this kind of social engineering, on a sunny Saturday I cannot help but be seduced by the simple beauty of it all—the children playing in the fountains, the clean lines and sharp corners, all that glass and granite. Everything as perfect as an artist's rendering of a city. No mess, no disorder, nothing to discomfort or interrupt me as I drift on the warm breeze. This is how they get you.

But it would be too easy to blame all of this on urban design. I am more than capable of finding my own ways to float out of reach of any unwanted interactions. For over twenty years now I have been wandering around towns and cities with various kinds of headphones on my head and music sluicing through my ears, drowning everything around me in a flood of invisible orchestration.

The first Sony Walkman was released in 1979 and became an instant phenomenon, selling fifty thousand units in its first two months. It represented a paradigm shift in our relationship to the surrounding environment—what Sony described as "headphone culture." Later inventions, in particular that of the iPod in 2001, would enable this culture to become more sophisticated and more pervasive; vast, private sound worlds accessed from a device so small you could forget you're even carrying it. According to a 2014 survey reported in *The New Yorker*, 53 per cent of adults between eighteen and thirty-four years old owned three or more pairs of headphones, and 73 per cent of those surveyed admitted to having used them to "avoid interaction with other people."

I could map out in music all the towns and cities I have walked through in my life. The way that Belle and Sebastian whistled plaintively through the grey Edinburgh streets of my late teenage years like melancholy birdsong. Or how *Boxer* by the National followed me like a marching band as, aged twenty-one, I freewheeled through Vancouver's Stanley Park in the dappled sunshine. Or how Death Grips appeared to erupt from the cobblestones of Bristol Harbour, rattling the disused cargo sheds and filling the air with the aluminium tang of electricity. Or just last year, hearing "Lark" by Angel Olsen for the first time as I walked through the too-polite streets of North London and feeling my heart swell to the size of a parade float. But all these places are phantoms—experienced and remembered by me and me alone. I have layered this music over the people and the situations that really make up those places, expunging them from my memory in the process.

At the same time, the headphones through which this music is pumped into my head serve as a clear indication to the rest of the world of my desire for privacy. As all those people surveyed in *The New Yorker* understood, wearing headphones outside is akin to hanging a "do not disturb" sign from your ears. Even when they don't actually block out the world around you, headphones give the wearer licence to ignore things they would rather not engage with by pretending that they cannot hear them or do not understand what it is taking place.

Of course, for many people navigating public space, this demand for privacy is a legitimate response to the hostility or harassment they have previously faced there. A convenient way of blocking out unwanted attention. Indeed, the "guy asking a woman to take her earbuds out" has become a kind of internet joke, emblematic of a particular category of overconfident man incapable of respecting other people's boundaries. But whilst headphones may provide a much-needed refuge from such attention, they also, inevitably, enable the wearer to cut themselves off from other kinds of encounters. They provide a way for people to extend their private space into public space, to wrap it around themselves like a blanket, for comfort and protection or even just for the sake of convenience.

Begging is the one kind of urban encounter more than any other that my headphones give me licence to ignore. There are lots of people who beg in London. This is perhaps unsurprising in a city where 50 per cent of the wealth is owned by the top 10 per cent and over a quarter of the population live below the poverty line. A city where one in every fifty-two people are homeless. And given that most people now carry a phone that provides them with directions, the time, and a means of calling someone in the case of an emergency, there are only a limited number of reasons why someone would approach a stranger and ask for their help. Asking for some spare change is the most common one.

In the past—for example, in theocratic and feudal societies without a well-developed welfare state—almsgiving was an important social function and begging was one useful strategy that the poor could employ to remind the rich and powerful of their obligations. Begging did not have a particular moral stigma attached to it, but failure to give certainly did. Today, however, in capitalist societies that valorise self-reliance and personal responsibility, the opposite could be said to be true. We have attached to begging a unique kind of shame, causing it to often appear at the very bottom of lists of the street-level economic activities that destitute people say they would engage in for their survival, below petty crimes such as drug dealing and theft.

Begging makes people deeply uncomfortable, and the feverish debate that persists about the genuineness of beggars is one way of attempting to project that discomfort onto the person who is doing the begging, casting them as the moral agent and the passer-by as a passive innocent ready to be taken advantage of; a "mark." But such hand-wringing about the legitimacy of the person begging is incidental to what is really happening in this encounter. The source of our discomfort runs much deeper.

Any instance of begging is a small encounter, as quiet and fleeting as any encounter can be—eyes briefly meeting and a few muttered words offered and returned, all in the space of no more than a handful of seconds—but nonetheless it glows white hot with meaning. It blisters and it burns. For the person begging, it is to risk rejection over and over again, whilst for the person whose help is being asked for, the encounter demands that they acknowledge the fractures that our social system usually insists are not their problem. It asks them to acknowledge an iniquity that should be almost unbearable. In doing so it may be thought of as precisely the kind of encounter with difference that makes our cities so important.

It can be hard to acknowledge such difference, in part because to do so can be so overwhelming. How do I help? What amount of help is enough? What can I personally do to resolve the fundamental inequities of my society so that people no longer have to beg strangers for change outside their local supermarket? The temptation is instead to look away, as I so often do. To avoid making any kind of moral judgement for fear of making an inadequate one, or even the wrong one.

But as Diane Arbus's photographs remind me, to encounter and acknowledge the things that separate us from one another is not the same as to presume we are capable of resolving those differences. Sometimes to merely bear witness to those divisions is enough. "She wanted to see the world whole," as writer Hilton Als puts it, "which meant seeing and accepting the fractures in those connections, too, along with all that could not be fixed." There is of course plenty that we could and should be doing to fix the social problems we see around us, but in the moment of that everyday human encounter, sometimes it is enough to sit with the difference and in doing so find a point of connection within it, however fractured that might be. To recognise the discomfort and know you cannot immediately make it go away.

The man outside the supermarket is still there, I think, but I see him much less these days. The pandemic created a separation from my old familiar routines, and I have not yet settled back into them. Perhaps I never will. I don't tend to go to the supermarket so often, and when I do, I don't have any change with me—I don't even have a wallet, instead using my phone to pay for my groceries. And so I find myself embarrassed to catch his eye and yet again apologise for having nothing for him. Recently I have caught myself avoiding him entirely. Nipping past without him noticing. With my headphones firmly lodged in my ears, it is so easy to float by with a nod of the head and some half-hearted gesture to indicate that today I can't help. Today I have nothing, sorry. Because I am in a hurry, I will reassure myself, or too preoccupied with some private worry or other to accommodate the interruption.

4. The Sissy

Nando Messias is a performance artist who lives in London. They have dark hair and thin, delicate features and they move like a chorus of birdsong, long limbs describing pretty patterns in the air with precise, understated grace. When Nando performs, they do so with a fabulousness that is intoxicating and an elegance that could cut glass.

I first saw Nando perform in a shoebox-sized theatre above a pub in West London. They performed a five-minute cabaret piece called "Walking Failure," appearing on the bare, black stage as a vision in white fur and red heart-shaped sunglasses, lip-syncing to a recording of the cultural theorist Judith Butler reflecting on a violent homophobic assault on an unnamed young man. Nando wrapped their body around each word as Butler describes the

46

swish of the young man's walk, the way his hips moved, and how this caused the other boys in his small town to abuse and eventually kill him. "Why," Butler asked, "would someone be killed for the way they walk? Why would that walk be so upsetting to those other boys that they would feel they must negate this person, that they must expunge the trace of that person, that they must stop that walk, no matter what?" And the question hung there, burnishing each movement with a fragile, transgressive power as Nando strutted across the stage and Butler's words looped over and over—"stop that walk, stop that walk, stop that walk."

This short performance was a direct response to a homophobic assault that Nando themselves experienced in their home city of London whilst walking home from a theatre in Whitechapel. Eight young men pushed Nando to the ground, punching and kicking them. "Once home," Nando writes, "I saw that my knees were bruised and so too was my pride. The torn veil and battered clutch went in the bin. My anger did not."

Throughout the performance, a series of red helium balloons were suspended from Nando's white fur coat. They floated there in the air as Nando sashayed from one side of the stage to the other, as if they were the cause of the lightness in each step, their gravity-defying affect allowing the bounce and the sway that made this walk so captivating, so balletic. As the short piece reached its climax Nando took out a staple gun and burst each balloon in turn. Each bang punched through the small auditorium until all the balloons were gone and Nando dropped to the floor, the lights went out, and we sat together in that silence. Finally, someone started clapping.

"Walking Failure" is a reminder, though many readers will not need one, that the difference we encounter on the streets of any city is not encountered equally by everybody. That in any given society there are some people who are marked as different and who therefore experience difference in perpetual fear of violence and exclusion.

In *Strange Encounters* the writer Sarah Ahmed makes the distinction between a stranger—that is, somebody we recognise *as strange*—and the people around us who we read not as strangers, but as people who are simply unknown to us; neighbours, kinfolk, other members of the community we are a part of. As Ahmed describes it, recognising someone *as a stranger* is an active process. It is not simply that we fail to recognise someone as familiar to us, it is that we recognise them as someone who is strange, *other*; someone who is different to the rest of us. In this sense, strangeness is not something that simply exists in the world. It is, rather, an effect that is constantly in the process of being reproduced. We recognise the strangeness of these strangers by reading it on their bodies—the colour of their skin or the way they walk, for example—and constitute our communities and our sense of belonging through the exclusion or the expulsion of those people who have been marked as strange.

It is on a city's streets that this process takes its most tangible form, rehearsed each and every day through tiny encounters that litter our streets like broken glass. Suspicious looks, tuts and eye rolls, muttered comments, jokes, insults, escalating to verbal abuse and physical violence. "The enforcement of boundaries," Ahmed writes, "requires that some-body—here locatable in the dirty figure of the stranger—has already crossed the line, has already come too close."

The question of who belongs on the streets of a city manifests itself in a variety of ways. The direction of violence and abuse towards marginalised bodies is one. Another is the harassment of women by men through sexualised comments, provocative gestures, honking, wolf-whistling, unwanted "compliments" intended to discomfort and humiliate their subjects. These too are a form of marking, another means of exclusion. As cities developed and the public and private spheres separated, in patriarchal societies women found themselves increasingly con-strained to the private, domestic sphere, with public space coded as male. Street harassment is an attempt to police this archaic separation. To assert to a woman that they do not have the right to belong here in the street, unless they are in search of male company or there to entertain the desires of men.

It is easy for me, as a straight white man, to write about the wondrous possibilities of encountering strangers on the streets of the city. In the cities where I have lived in the UK and in Can-ada, I have had the privilege of being unmarked by difference and of never having my right to inhabit public space questioned. I have only a limited understanding of what it feels like for the experience of walking in public space to be freighted with the very real threat of violence and harassment, and how this might colour one's relationship to the encounters one has there. But to see Nando Messias reperform the violence inflicted upon them simply for the way they walk, or to share in the grief and anger that accompanies yet another incident of racialised or gendered violence on the streets of my own city, or just to witness the myriad everyday harassments that make my experience of walking around in London different to that of my partner, all of it is enough for anyone to recognise that we do not yet share in the same right to the city.

Part of the remedy to the intersecting exclusions that compromise so many people's experiences of public space must be sought beyond the streets, through attempting to resolve the larger prejudices and inequalities that fracture our societies. But there are also things that can and are being done out on the streets themselves. We can all of us begin to change who is marked as strange and who is recognised as a neighbour through our everyday interactions with the people around us. There are ways of finding new connections through the blizzard of conflicts and collisions that so often constitute an experience of public space. Moments of encounter in which we can begin to better understand the complexity of our differences and find, despite or because of them, points of continuity and mutual recognition. We can all be a part of creating that increasingly rare thing in public space, congregation.

Three years after I first saw Nando Messias perform in that tiny space in West London, I was in a much larger, grander theatre on the other side of town, watching them perform again. Again the trauma of the assault they had experienced was at the centre of the piece. The show began in the theatre, with Nando nearly naked in a pool of light whilst a group of unsmiling men in tuxedos lingered menacingly in the shadows. But in the show's second act we were escorted out of the auditorium into a cobbled alleyway behind the theatre, where the men had become a marching band and the audience a parade. We all followed in Nando's wake as they marched past the exact spot where the assault had taken place, reclaiming their place on the streets in what they described as a "hyperbolic display of visibility." Sky-blue ballgown and matching fur, red high heels, and a festoon of bright balloons.

Bystanders looked on in confusion and astonishment and people peered from the top deck of buses as we gathered in a nearby square for a re-enactment of the original incident, transformed into a wordless musical ballet performed by Nando and their tuxedoed marching band. A tragicomic remaking of private horror as communal spectacle. It was a gathering that did not erase Nando's fabulous strangeness; indeed, it actively championed it. Nor did it gloss over the violence they experienced in pursuit of some sentimental celebration of community. The performance was still bruised and bruising, but it sought out a path through that pain towards connection and communion. In doing so it became an act of reclamation; of the streets, of the night, of the city itself. All it might be and all it might one day allow us to be.

5. A Snowball Fight in East London

Cities are frequently so big these days, and the people in them so fragmented, that there are few things left that can interrupt everybody all at once, but weather is one of them. It can snarl up the traffic or stop it completely, close public buildings, leave people running for cover or spilling out into the street. Even today, in a world of seemingly infinite distractions, a sudden burst of unexpected weather is still a spectacle. An experience that transforms the city around us and our relationship to it, even if only temporarily.

In his short story "Spring Rain," John Updike describes a rainstorm in New York City as a whirl of movement and colour. Water squeezing through the gaps in the corridors of buildings, dribbling down the edges of awnings, and swirling and eddying in the gutters. Amidst this tumult, bodies rush for cover, transforming the city into a patchwork of shelters—"a mobile conglomerate of dabs of dryness swimming through a fabric of wet."

A good rainstorm changes the geography of a place, "exquisitely pressing the city down into itself," as Updike describes it. It simplifies things. In ordinary circumstances a busy street is a kaleidoscope of journeys and intentions, so many different realities struggling past one another, jostling for space on the pavement. But in a rainstorm there is, briefly, just rain and the need for shelter. In making the city strange, a rainstorm has the potential to temporarily upset our preconceptions of who belongs in a place and who doesn't. It can transform us from a scrum of contradictory individuals into common bodies seeking sanctuary from the wet.

It can be so exhilarating, squeezed together in the entrance-way of a covered arcade or under a café awning, watching the rain fall out of the sky. From the safety of our shelter we watch together the rain falling in sheets around us, sympathising with those unlucky people who are late to find safety from the weather as they dry their glasses on a patch of T-shirt and shake the water from their hair. The relationships between strangers are redrawn by this weather. Our differences washed away for a few moments, at least, by the shared need to evade the downpour.

Away from these places of temporary refuge, out there in the shower, there is another kind of solidarity that exists between those brave few who have ventured out, sharing defiant nods and wry smiles from beneath their umbrellas or the tightly tied hoods of their raincoats as they walk on through the puddles. Children splash and dogs shiver, and we shrug on through the downpour.

Such a suspension of the normal rules of encounter is only ever fleeting. The rain passes and people quickly disperse. In "Spring Rain," Updike describes how the "crowds that had been clustered in entranceways and under overhangs shattered and scattered like drying pods." Weather of this kind normally comes and goes in a matter of minutes, and the encounters we are able to have within it are therefore short and limited— acknowledgements of a shared predicament, commiserations on being outside in such inhospitable conditions.

But other kinds of weather can last longer and create different kinds of encounters. In New York in the hottest days of summer, the caps have been coming off fire hydrants since 1896 as a way to cool down amidst the hot concrete, creating a temporary, semi-authorised suspension of the normal operation of a city street in the process. In Spike Lee's *Do the Right Thing*, for example, the uncapping of a fire hydrant creates a temporary respite from the intensity that will eventually consume the Bed-Stuy street on which the film is set. Holding a broken tin can over the stream of water, two young men create a fountain under which people gather to laugh and wrestle, their clothes soaked through. For a moment the broiling tensions of the heatwave are nearly forgotten as people rush out into the street to play.

In London the heatwaves tend to be rarer and less severe, and though a warm day will bring people flocking to the city's many parks, there is no equivalent takeover of its streets. Instead the thing that has always brought people out in London is the snow.

In the period known as the Little Ice Age, between about 1650 and 1850, the Thames would regularly freeze over and Londoners from all walks of life would spill out onto the ice to skate and eat and play. They called it Freezeland Street—a new, temporary destination in the bustling metropolis. People would build booths selling various kinds of food and drink. Attractions would appear, crude carousels made of boats attached to poles and swung around in a circle. Even King Charles II was seen venturing out onto the ice to visit the frost fair. In Abraham Hondius's painting *The Frozen Thames* from 1677, the river is transformed into an Arctic tundra, tiny figures scrambling delightedly over great blocks of ice. In the distance London Bridge, Southwark Cathedral, and all the city's ordinary concerns wait quietly. For now, though, we are in another world.

As the weather has warmed it tends to snow less and less in London. I have lived here for over fifteen years and I can remember only a handful of proper snow days, when the weather still causes the city's merciless gears to stop whirring. Days when the Underground stops running and the streets empty of buses and cars, when the parks sparkle brilliant white like bedsheets drying in the sun. Days when the normal rules that govern how we relate to each other and the world around us are suspended just long enough that we are able to imagine new ones.

On the night of February 1, 2009, I was at a flat in East London with some friends, drinking wine and letting time get away from us in the way that it is sometimes possible to do when you have nothing much to get up for the next day. It was after midnight when we noticed that it was snowing, and not just the kind of thin, begrudging snow that London normally gets—this was blizzardy fists of white dropping out of the sky like a system error. We threw on our coats and ran out into the street.

On the grubby high street the snow was already several inches thick. The city felt soft and heavy, like someone had wrapped it in a duvet. Buses and taxis tiptoed through greying slush, and on the corner of Kingsland Road and Richmond Road a snowball fight had broken out among an array of people you might expect to meet on an East London street in the early hours of the morning: gangs of local teenagers, inebriated nightclub revellers, people who just happened to be walking home. Between the flurries of snow and the coats and hoods people were wrapped up in, it was hard to make out who anyone was. At its peak there were perhaps twenty-five people fanned out across both sides of the street, using parked cars as temporary barricades, scooping up the fresh snow and packing it down with red, raw hands. People emerged from passing buses and immediately joined the fray. Others drove by in cars, slowing down to hurl snowballs from the rear window.

It was undoubtedly the best snowball fight I have ever been a part of, a snowball fight for the ages. The kind of snowball fight that deserved its own orchestrated accompaniment. That deserves its own special on the History Channel. By the second hour, what had started as a practical joke had become a piece of euphoric, durational group choreography; a hole in the normal functioning of the world that we all poured ourselves into. The Thames may not freeze over any more, but for one night at least Freezeland had returned, the city shivered to a stop, and we all skated out onto the ice. Our differences forgotten in a giddy avalanche of play.

I think about this night every time I walk down that grubby high street. In some small way it transformed my relationship to the entire street and all the people I see there; each of them now a potential player, past or future. When I walk there, I walk lightly because I know that under the paving stones there is nothing but freshly fallen snow.

6. A Circle of Bicycles

Every night in the small English town of St Helens, a group of teenagers ride around on their bikes in the town centre. They ride around because there is nothing else to do. Many of the shops are boarded up. There are virtually no youth centres. With no other spaces to occupy, they keep moving, cycling in endless circles. Because they are cycling it is hard to approach them, even if you wanted to. Many of the other people moving through this space say they are intimidated by them, but that is not the teenagers' problem, and anyway perhaps it is part of the point.

Ask children what improvements they would like to make to the towns and cities they live in, and in my experience the thing they will usually tell you is that they want more places to play. In 2021 my partner, Beckie, and I worked with around 150 primary school children in St Helens, helping them to create their own guidebook to the town as a way for adults to see and understand it through their eyes. As part of the creation of this *Book of St Helens*, we asked the children what changes they would like to make to the streets they lived on, and the answer we got over and over again was more places to play.

They imagined adventure playgrounds, elaborate constructions with tyre swings, mini ground trampolines, tunnel slides, and climbing nets. They told us about rock-climbing walls and paintball woods. New football pitches that weren't perpetually muddy and had nets so that they didn't have to run and collect the ball every time a goal was scored. They wanted an underwater exploration park with a marine zip line across a body of water, and a mermaid and an underwater slide. A petting zoo and a city farm. A bug hotel and a community garden. Most of the children's suggestions were not all that practical ("a rollercoaster held up by a wall of living plants that absorbs carbon dioxide to help stop pollution"), but all of them spoke to something fundamental that they had recognised about the streets of their town. There was not enough space in which to play.

According to Dr Maarten Koeners, founder of the Playful University Club at Exeter University, play is not simply something we do to pass the time, it is an essential physiological process, akin to sleep. When adult rats are deprived of the opportunity to play and then reintroduced to their playmates, they play significantly more to catch up with the play that they missed, in the same way they might sleep more to catch up on sleep. Through play we learn how to imbue our everyday interactions with greater compassion. It is a means through which we learn to live better in the world.

When the snow fell over London back in 2019 my first instinct was to play, just as it was the first instinct for those New Yorkers each summer who gathered in the shimmering spray of an uncapped water hydrant. But the weather cannot always be relied upon to provide opportunities for adults to reconnect with their younger selves and relearn to play together on the streets of their cities. It requires more regular and more strategic interventions.

Some of these interventions may involve the use of digital technology. The same devices that have been so effective at displacing us into our own private auditory universes are also increasingly being used to bring people together to play out on the streets of their towns and cities. The best-known example is Pokémon Go, an augmented-reality game that encouraged players to explore the world around them in order to capture and train digital creatures attached to real locations. In the fever-dream summer of 2016, Pokémon Go became an omnipresent cultural phenomenon, downloaded over 500 million times by the end of the year, causing congregations of players to appear seemingly at random in unlikely locations, gathering in awkward bunches, eyes darting between their phones and the surrounding environment in search of new creatures or locations where they could train them.

Pokémon Go got millions of people out and about, playing in the streets, but in doing so it also created a notoriously fraught relationship between those users and the world around them, with stories abounding of players walking obliviously out into the middle of busy roads, falling off cliffs, or traipsing through people's private gardens in search of their quarry. Any game of this nature is fundamentally a mediated encounter with the world and the people in it. And invariably when we allow technology companies to mediate our encounters in this way, the priorities and preconceptions of those companies influence how we end up interacting. Some people get left out, difference is flattened by scale, and our potential for compassion is overridden by the priorities of the software itself.

Instead I am instinctively drawn to simpler, less explicitly game-like forms of play. Play that looks like nothing more than curiosity, creating opportunities for anyone to gently and playfully renegotiate their relationships to the people and the world around them. Projects like *Radio Local*, an artwork by artists Jenny Hunt and Holly Darton that took the form of a pop-up local radio station, which appeared in towns and cities across the UK in 2018 and 2019.

Dressed in matching costumes with radio antennae strapped to their heads, the artists would set up their open-air radio studio right in the middle of the high street, using their bright costumes and the offer of a cup of tea and a biscuit as a way of encouraging passers-by to stop and involve themselves in the making of this unlikely day-long broadcast. Starting with virtually nothing, the artists would rely on the passers-by to fill their programming, asking them to record radio jingles in a specially designed shed, write and perform storylines for a do-it-yourself soap opera, or take part in made-up game shows, such as asking people to fill dead air by talking for a minute without stopping about a subject whose name they couldn't mention; and so an eight-year-old trying to describe death might be followed by a pensioner explaining what Subway is. At the end of every broadcast, everyone the artists had interacted with throughout the day was invited back for a celebratory summing up. Awards were handed out, toasts were made, and the DIY soap opera was performed by and for the assembled crowd of strangers.

At its heart *Radio Local* is a kind of interruption, an attempt to temporarily reconfigure the way we use our streets. Jenny and Holly have become masters of managing the tension and awkwardness that our unfamiliar co-presence in these spaces often leads to. Like Diane Arbus, they are willing to sit with the discomfort of our differences until something new blooms out of them. "The good thing about giving people a cup of tea," Jenny tells me over the phone, "is that it takes a little while to drink, and by the time you've done so, people feel comfortable enough to hang around and take part further."

Another part of the broadcast involved Jenny and Holly conducting impromptu restaurant reviews by inviting proprietors from all local cafés and restaurants to bring food out into the street to be judged by the artists and their volunteer helpers. In doing so they recreate in microcosm the kind of bustling street life that would have been the norm back in the long-distant past when the city street was the locus of everything and the boundaries between public realm and private business were so much more porous.

In June 2019 Hunt and Darton brought their radio station to St Helens, setting up their makeshift studio on a high street littered with shuttered shops and bright neon posters advertising going-out-of-business sales. As the afternoon wore on, the teenagers appeared on their bikes, ready to resume their nightly occupation of this space. Initially hostile to having to share the street with this temporary art installation, they cycled in circles round and round the radio station. But Jenny and Holly welcomed them as they do everyone, offering them tea and biscuits and giving them the chance to be contestants in their radio game show. As dusk arrived, the teenagers were still there, bikes splayed out on the ground, all of them now part of the congregation of people standing together to perform their own ramshackle radio soap opera.

Teenagers, pensioners, families, neighbours, and strangers, their divisions not mended by any means, but sharing this space for now, finding a way to coexist, playing together as the day slipped away and the street lights blinked on one by one.

CHAPTER 3

A SHORT HISTORY OF NOT
GOING OUT

Part 1: Talking on the Phone

Imagine we are talking on the telephone. What can you know about me?

This is the sound of my voice. It is a voice with an English accent. The voice of someone who is approximately thirty (?) or maybe forty years old. It is a deepish voice, louder than a voice needs to be. There may be small clues in the way I speak that enable you to guess where I grew up or make assumptions about the kind of school I went to (assumptions which may or may not be right). I may sound like I have a cold or a cough. I may sound out of breath.

In the background you might be able to hear a chatter of voices, leading you to deduce that I am in a café or a restaurant or shop. An announcement over a public address system could give away that I am in an airport or a railway station. The noise of traffic or even birdsong could let you know that I am outside. You might hear the quality of my voice change as I move from a large room to a small one, and any awkward pauses or muffled bluster could lead you to believe that I am distracted by trying to do something else at the same time as speaking to you— answering emails maybe or making dinner or walking the dog.

You cannot know how tall I am. You cannot tell the colour of my eyes. You cannot judge the clothes I am wearing or the way I sit with my legs crossed just so. You cannot tell if I am smiling or how many other people are sitting quietly nearby, listening in.

You cannot know what I was just doing. You cannot know what I am in the middle of doing. If you were to call me on my landline, you might assume you know where I am, but even that assumption could for a number of reasons be wrong. In so many ways, any encounter that you and I have over the telephone is an encounter that is defined by unknowing.

• • •

There is something quite wonderful about an invention that brings us closer together at the same time as reminding us how far apart we are. It is a kind of seduction. Or like a promise from a fairy tale. A wish only partially fulfilled. This magical device will cast a spell and grant you the chance to meet, but your meetings will be forever shrouded in darkness.

As is usually the case in a good fairy tale, this outcome is pleasure laced with pain. Happiness forestalled. But then the telephone has always been associated with a kind of longing. Connection framed by absence creating a desire for human contact that cannot be satisfied through this contraption alone. The very first words spoken down a telephone line (by Alexander Graham Bell to his assistant in the neighbouring room) were "Mr. Watson—come here—I want to see you."

How many people in the 150 years since then have cried forlornly into their telephone, wishing they could see or touch or be with the person on the other end of the line?

In Marie Cartier's book *Baby, You Are My Religion* she tells the story of Myrna Kurland, a queer woman who used to frequent gay bars and dated a professional women's softball player during the 1940s. After the war ended Myrna felt pressured to marry and have children. She married a psychiatrist who believed homosexuality was a mental illness, so she was forced to hide her sexuality for fear of being sent away and losing her children. During frequent bouts of insomnia she would sit up late into the night, calling the gay bars she remembered so fondly from her earlier life, sitting silently on the end of the line just to listen. "I would just hear the noise and laughter in the background," she said. "I just wanted to be there."

● ● ●

Proximity and distance—the feeling of being so close and yet so far away—creates, in the telephone call, a bewitching kind of intimacy. A closeness that cannot be experienced in any other way.

Bell called his invention "talk with electricity" and anyone who has stayed up too late talking on the phone with an old lover or a new lover or a prospective lover would surely agree with him. The handset cradled against your ear. The voice on the other end of the line so close. Closer than it could ever decently be face to face. ASMR before we had a word for it.

Hollywood has often used this special quality of intimacy in a telephone call to good effect. Especially during the era of the Hays Code, when actually showing a couple in a sexual situation together was strictly forbidden. A split screen telephone call could provide a kind of intimacy that the audience weren't allowed to access in any other way.

There is a scene, for example, in the 1959 film *Pillow Talk* in which Doris Day and Rock Hudson are talking on the phone. Each is sitting in the bath. We see them both in split screen, the two rooms perfectly aligned so that the couple seem to lie at opposite ends of the same (extra-long) bath. They talk together softly about nothing in particular, giggling occasionally. This gentleness feels transgressive in more ways than one. At one point Rock Hudson lifts his foot up, placing it against the bathroom wall, only for Doris Day to do the same a few seconds later so that their feet appear to be touching.

There they sit, whispering right into each other's ears. Two voices, each freighted with just the right amount of longing, talking to each other through the darkness.

• • •

When I was seventeen I fell madly in love with a girl called Sofia on a two-week-long cultural exchange to the Spanish city of Zaragoza. We kissed goodbye by my school bus and promised we'd be together forever, or at least the next few weeks. The phone calls that followed were long and expensive. We would talk and talk and when we couldn't think of anything else to say to one another, we would sit in silence and play each other our favourite songs down the line. This, more than anything else, is what I remember from these phone calls—listening so intently as she held the handset in front of the CD player, focusing as much on the sound of her breathing as the music she was playing for me.

I think the telephone might be the greatest medium we currently have for expressing love. An exchange of love letters might be romantic in a sentimental, nostalgic kind of way, but it doesn't really embody all of love's fervour and its anxiety, all that awkwardness, that uncertainty and that longing, in the same way a telephone call can. And not just romantic love.

My brother once called me in the middle of the night just to tell me he loved me. He was unfathomably high, wandering the streets of Liverpool with a friend of his. Through our teenage years we could barely say two words to each other without starting an argument, but here he was at one in the morning, telling me what it meant to be a brother and asking me what drugs I'd tried. After a while I told him I had to go because my phone battery was running down and I didn't have a charger (which was true). He told me I needed to wake up one of my flatmates to use their phone. This phone call was too important not to. "Because I'm your brother," he told me, "and I love you."

And then there is every call I've ever had with my grandmother in Florida, each of which goes exactly the same way. "Hello, my darling," she says, "how are you?" I tell her I'm good, and then without fail she tells me how hot it has been that day, how beautiful it is, how much the sun is shining. I tell her how cold it is in London and how grey. Then she reiterates that it really is so nice there today, that the sky is blue and she is already out in the garden. She laughs at the absurdity of it, the gap between these two places, the tropical paradise she lives in now and the strange little island she once called home. I tell her I need to visit her soon and she agrees with her whole heart, her voice as bright and as warm as the Florida weather.

Love is the phone call in the middle of the night, when feeling has overwhelmed you and you have no option but to share it. But love is also the comforting sense of proximity that the telephone provides us with the rest of the time; those calls home on a Sunday afternoon, the five-minute catch-up whilst waiting for the bus, the call you make on the walk home despite the fact you'll see each other face to face in only a few minutes' time.

• • •

On the telephone we listen attentively, wrapping ourselves around each other's voices. We hold on tight to what we can know and allow ourselves to imagine the rest.

But any encounter that withholds so much from its participants requires trust and is open to exploitation. If you cannot know where the person you are speaking to is, who they are with, what they are doing, or even who they actually are, you may have legitimate grounds to be suspicious of their intentions. Perhaps even to be afraid of them.

"Do you like scary movies?" asks the sinister voice on the telephone to Drew Barrymore at the beginning of the 1996 film *Scream*.

Their encounter begins harmlessly enough. A seemingly wrong number that, it quickly becomes apparent, is no such thing. The male voice on the line is soft-spoken and flirtatious, but the conversation jackknifes suddenly when he tells her he wants to know her name because "I want to know who I'm looking at."

It is chilling, this moment of realisation. An encounter that appeared to be one thing has in a flash been revealed to be something else entirely. All our encounters over the telephone are defined by an expectation of symmetry: we cannot see each other, cannot know what the other is doing. It is a kind of unspoken contract—a trust we rely on to navigate through the darkness. But here that trust is broken. Now all the power and all the knowledge sit at one end of the line.

You don't have to end up being brutally murdered to find

these circumstances unbearable. At one point in the late 1990s my parents started receiving prank phone calls. The phone would ring, and when we picked it up the call would connect but no one would say anything. You could hear the sound of a room somewhere, imagine a person holding the phone, their face an agonising blank. Each time we answered the call we would fall into a void. Soon after it began, my parents changed their number and went ex-directory. We never discovered where the calls were coming from.

• • •

A lot of people are afraid of talking on the phone, and not just those that have watched too many horror movies. Telephobia is a recognised condition, and an understandable one.

On a telephone call there are no social cues to guide or reassure you and none of the shared distractions that cushion our everyday face-to-face conversations—a coffee to stir, a window to look out of, a passing world to walk through or observe. You cannot compensate for nerves with energy or affection, or try to take your social cues from the person sitting opposite you.

There are only these voices, this naked back and forth of listening and being listened to. Everything else is stripped away.

In this vacuum, you are required to improvise. Your words are offered up for intimate, unseen scrutiny at the very moment they tumble from your mouth. You cannot spend hours or even days preparing exactly the right wording to make your meaning clear, nor can you rephrase something or take it back entirely if you see it causing a wince of discomfort or an uncomprehending look from the person you are speaking with.

A conversation on the telephone can feel like a high-wire act with the safety net removed. We scramble anxiously towards understanding without the encouragement of a smile or a nodding face. Feeling our way gingerly forward through all this empty space, caught in the glare of the spotlight, worried that one wrong foot will send us crashing to the floor.

It can all be so awkward, so static, so constrained. It is all just too unbearably close.

● ● ●

There are some phone calls that feel too close, and then there are some phone calls that don't feel close at all.

As more and more people acquired telephones, there developed a need for a mechanism to ensure that the right people were being connected to one another. At first this was the job of switchboard operators, diligent telephonic cupids whose job it was to physically connect one person to another via series of switches and cables—completing the circuit that allowed this electric conversation to happen.

Later, callers would be able to use a rotary dial or a number pad to connect themselves to the person they wanted to speak to via a system called direct dialling. Whilst the technology had changed, the intention was still the same—one person who desired to speak to another would pick up the phone and call them in the hope that a connection would be made.

Then, in the 1950s, a new piece of technology was created that changed everything. It was called an automated call distributor. This device made it possible to sort large numbers of incoming calls automatically, without the need for an operator or a receptionist. An algorithm assesses the calls, using either information from the caller ("If you are calling about an existing problem, please press 1"), or information about the caller determined by their telephone number, or the time of day the call was processed or a combination of all three, and then assigns the call to an appropriate agent or network of agents.

What resulted was an entirely new category of telephonic encounter. No longer did there need to be any human connection between the person calling and the person answering. Now the two can be randomly assigned to each other by a computer. Strangers thrown together by the whims of the machine gods.

• • •

By the late 1970s and early 1980s the automatic call distributor had spawned the modern call centre. Vast strip-lit warehouses full of anonymous agents in telephone headsets, fielding a never-ending stream of decontextualised inquiries, often from callers in a completely different country.

Here, the unknowing that defines any interaction over the telephone is exploited to create encounters of profound asymmetry and absence. Call centre workers in New Delhi are trained to adopt Westernised names and neutralise their accents. Sex line operators, working from a vast converted Toys "R" Us store in

South Florida, feign whatever set of physical characteristics the caller had input a preference for.

In this new reality, the connection between one end of the line and the other is so opaque it leads to a kind of depersonalisation. The speakers become anonymous nodes moving around inside a network they can't control and don't understand. Resolving bugs and fulfilling tasks like they're lines of computer code. Here in microcosm is the grand arc of capitalism itself—the reduction of human interaction down to its most basic components so that they may more efficiently serve the interests of capital.

As most of us have experienced at one time or other, the actual human encounter at the centre of all of this machinery can be fraught and unpleasant. It is too easy to reduce the person at the other end of the line to little more than a voice to scream at through the void. According to a recent survey conducted in the US, 81 per cent of call centre workers had received abuse from customers, and over a third had been threatened with violence, which helps explain why call centres have one of the highest staff turnover rates of any industry.

● ● ●

A friend of mine spent several years working in a call centre for one of the UK's network of private railway companies—answering calls from people wanting to purchase train tickets. She told me she got used to most interactions ending in being hung up on, if not worse, but that she learnt quickly that the way to make the experience bearable was to latch onto those callers who seemed to want to talk, stretching those conversations out for as long as possible. If she ended up talking to the right kind of elderly lady, between them they could make the process of buying train tickets last for several hours. From her desk in a giant room in an anonymous retail park in the North East of England, she would talk with those voices on the other end of the phone about their lives. Meandering conversations about everything and nothing that exploited the very programmes designed to eliminate such glorious inefficiency.

Something similar is taking place in the German theatre company Rimini Protokoll's 2008 project *Call Cutta in a Box*—a piece they describe as an "intercontinental phone play." In the performance, a single audience member standing alone in an empty office is invited to pick up a ringing phone and begin a conversation with a call centre worker in Calcutta, recruited by the theatre company and working, temporarily, as a performer from the same call centre desk where they would normally field customer service inquiries from other unseen and faraway callers. In this staid environment a conversation begins that transgresses all the normal conventions of this kind of functional encounter. The call centre worker introduces themselves to the audience member and initiates an intimate conversation about the distance between them and the very different lives they lead. They talk together about love and work and the complex relationships of commerce and labour that have brought them together, in the process rendering visible so much that normally remains hidden.

Both these examples in their very different ways show how this alienating apparatus can be repurposed. That the randomness and dislocation built into the automated machinery of the call centre can be usurped and remade. That even these calls can become encounters of genuine meaning and connection.

And really, a telephone should always allow for this possibility. You don't need to be taking part in a piece of interactive theatre to turn a routine phone call into a genuine conversation. Any call, no matter how mundane or anonymous, is still rooted in that familiar back and forth of listening and being listened to. There is still some electricity there, no matter how faint. It is still a place in which anything can happen.

But perhaps not for much longer.

• • •

Was it text messaging that finally killed the telephone call? Was it email? Was it the robocaller? Automated customer service? MSN Messenger? Was it Facebook or Snapchat? Instagram? Was it Skype? Zoom? Microsoft Teams? Was it Drew Barrymore? Was it prank calling? Was it scary movies? Was it telephobia? The changing social habits of millennials and Gen Zers? Was it automation? Artificial intelligence? The relentless drive for greater economic efficiency? Was it every company that conceals their customer support line in the depths of their website, beneath an array of nudges directing us instead towards online chat boxes, pages of frequently asked questions, and "Contact Us" forms?

Was it Apple and Samsung and the other smartphone designers, when their handsets became primarily devices for watching, reading, touching, and taking photographs, rather than for listening and speaking? Devices that in fact are not actually that convenient for making phone calls and certainly not as pleasant to hold cupped to your ear as a traditional landline phone whose curved plastic handset hugs close to your face like it's leaning in to tell you a secret.

The telephone has been dying for a long time and it is possible to diagnose many causes.

Writing in the *Atlantic* in 2015, Ian Bogost makes a convincing case for the primary cause being the telephone itself, or more specifically the shift from landlines to mobile phones.

Conventionally, a landline call functioned by linking two handsets to each other through an electric circuit made by a series of switches. This infrastructure is stable and dependable, usually binding the two speakers together as reliably as two tin cans connected by a piece of string. Mobile phones, on the other hand, operate on a cellular network that bounces calls through a series of transceivers positioned on rooftops and cell towers and consequently, as we have all experienced, the quality of these calls can vary wildly.

Over time we have become inured to the idea of phone calls being frustrating and unreliable. In movies and TV, phone calls are forever dropping out at the critical moment, the voices becoming garbled and incomprehensible. When I call my mum, she stands in the bedroom of her house and I stand in the kitchen of mine; otherwise we can't hear one another. A phone call never used to be like this.

Added to this, Bogost describes how in the 1960s, for the sake of efficiency, the bandwidth of a telephone call was shrunk to a narrow frequency range called the voice band, which eliminated higher frequencies to focus specifically on what were thought to be the frequencies crucial to human speech. In the process, however, we lose important elements of the human voice contained in those higher frequencies. This isn't a problem when your phone call is taking place in the quiet of a living room, an office, or a phone booth. But when one or the other of the callers is out and about in the world, the low-frequency background noise of a coffee shop or the hum of traffic can clash with the limited version of the human voice that a telephone call transmits, causing us to have to strain effortfully to listen and speak to one another. This too never used to be a part of our experience of a phone call—the effort, the exhaustion, all those "hellos" and "can you hear mes."

This is the great tragedy of the telephone in the twenty-first century. A familiar tale of hubris and ambition. By wanting to be everywhere all the time, the phone call lost the very qualities that made it so special in the first place.

● ● ●

Doris Day is standing awkwardly by the window, a towel wrapped hastily around her. She shakes her head and checks her phone, unsure if the problem is her reception or his.

Rock Hudson is in a cab, but he's about to go into a tunnel.

Doris Day is having lunch on the Upper West Side. Her phone sits on the table in front of her whilst she picks through a Caesar salad. She sees the screen light up with a picture of a smiling Rock Hudson in a Stetson. She considers answering, but the restaurant is loud and anyway she has other things she ought to be doing. She lets it silently ring out.

Rock Hudson is lying on his sofa, scrolling through Instagram whilst the TV plays in the background. He is wondering about the world and how we know so much about it these days. Too much about everything and everyone. He is thinking about the value of not knowing.

Doris Day is leaving a voice note and Rock Hudson is leaving her one back. Their words arrive like little parcels waiting to be unwrapped. They speak each parcel into their phones and then listen back carefully, rerecording when they deem it necessary, before finally pressing send. It is a conversation composed of fragments, constructed line by line like the dialogue in a play.

Rock Hudson is listening to Miles Davis with the window open, the notes tumbling out of the speaker in dizzying, unpredictable patterns. He remembers hearing Davis describe improvisation as the freedom and space to hear things. Lying on his sofa, Rock thinks about all those freewheeling late-night phone calls he and Doris once shared. How they felt like jazz. He remembers all the unexpected things they allowed him to hear.

Doris Day found out a while ago that Rock was not who

78

he claimed to be. He was no wealthy Texas rancher, he was a playboy composer who lived just down the block. She let his text messages go unread, and he quickly stopped sending them. They both carried on with their lives.

Now Rock Hudson is ordering an old fashioned and watching the twenty-four-hour news on a television in the corner of the bar whilst his phone buzzes away on the table in front of him. He is thinking longingly about the concept of mystery.

Doris Day has her out-of-office message on. She does not want to be disturbed. She lights a candle and sinks into the bath.

When are we just being nostalgic, she wonders, and when is something valuable really being lost?

• • •

In the midst of a global pandemic, a funny thing happened. People started using the telephone again.

In April 2020 the *New York Times* reported that Verizon were handling around 800 million calls a day, more than double the amount they would normally expect on even the busiest calling days of the year. Not only this, but the length of calls had risen by around a third from the average prior to COVID-19, significantly outpacing the increase in internet usage during the same period.

The article goes on to quote Jessica Rosenworcel, a commissioner at the Federal Communications Commission: "We've become a nation that calls like never before," she says. "We are craving human voice."

I'm sure this is true. I know there have been many times during that two years when I appreciated the comfort of a familiar voice on the other end of a telephone line. A simple, direct connection amidst so much isolation and upheaval, so many online meetings and socially distanced events. Two voices bound around one another, blocking out the noise of the world.

But I also like to think there is more to it than just this basic craving. In a time of such profound uncertainty, it makes sense to me that we would turn towards a medium that asks that we give up our desire to control. That we open ourselves up to the spontaneity and unpredictability that text and email fail to provide, and in doing so give ourselves the freedom and the space to really hear things. And that we would turn to a medium defined by its very limitedness. Voices luxuriating in darkness. A reminder of the fact that sometimes less really can be more.

My hope is that our rekindled love affair with the telephone can continue for many years to come. After all, the world is only growing darker and more confusing. Our lives more fragmented. We need a device in our pocket to invite us to reach out into the unknown, initiating encounters full of curiosity and longing. Talk with electricity.

• • •

There are any number of ways to hang up at the end of a telephone call.

You could, for example, do it like they do in the movies, without a thank you or a goodbye or any kind of niceties at all, slipping your phone neatly into your jacket pocket and striding purposefully towards the next scene.

Alternatively you could end it on your knees, like the unnamed woman at the centre of Jean Cocteau's play *The Human Voice*, intoning "I love you" over and over and over again into the handset.

You could hang up the call as I once did, at the end of a long and drunken argument, by simply throwing your phone across a park, for want of a switch hook to slam it down onto.

Or perhaps you are lucky enough to have a phone with a switch hook, in which case you can take great satisfaction cutting the call short by punching the handset into the little plastic button like a guillotine chop through your connection to the person on the other end.

You could accidentally drop your phone into a lake or a canal or a portable toilet, watching it float there helplessly for a few seconds before it disappears forever.

You could just say goodbye.

Or you could choose not to hang up at all, waiting instead for your partner on the other end to do so first.

And maybe they will or maybe they won't.

Maybe you'll both sit on the line in silence for a moment, listening for the sound of breathing, before one or the other of you presses a button and the line finally cuts out.

Part 2: Video Calling

In 1885, so the story goes, Jules Verne was asked by James Gordon Bennett Jr, owner of the *New York Herald* newspaper, to imagine life a thousand years in the future. His subsequent short story was eventually published four years later in the *Forum* magazine. For many years the story was credited solely to Jules Verne, but it is now generally considered to have been written primarily by his son, Michel Verne, employing many of his father's ideas.

"In the Year 2889" tells the story of a day in the life of the future media baron Fritz Napoleon Smith, technological innovator, loving husband, owner of the revolutionary *Earth Chronicle* newspaper, and possessor of what the Vernes describe as the "almost unimaginable" fortune of $10,000,000,000. To the Vernes' original readers, Fritz Napoleon Smith would be a familiar type. He might have been inspired by James Gordon Bennett Jr or by Joseph Pulitzer, who only six years earlier had bought the struggling *New York World* and begun turning around its fortunes. Equally, the Vernes might have just been reflecting more generally the flavour of the times. A faith in the benevolence and capability of these titans of business. These innovators. These leaders of men. Figures of seriousness and status who work every hour God sends them, with personalities powerful enough to reshape whole nations and divert the path of history itself.

But the point of the story is not to be a hagiography of this imagined newspaper magnate and his present-day contemporaries. Rather the story of Fritz Napoleon Smith is a device to enable the Vernes to introduce us to their vision of the future and to the many wonders of this unfathomable new age. They describe a world of limitless energy, harvested from the sun, water, and wind. Year-round agriculture made possible by storing up heat in the summer to be used to warm the winters. Cities of unprecedented scale—up to (just imagine it) ten million inhabitants. The average human lifespan extended from thirty-seven to fifty-two years. Advertisements projected onto the undersides of clouds. A plan to deliberately melt the polar ice caps to create vast new territories for habitation and resource extraction. The air cleansed of all microorganisms, ensuring the people of the future would "know nothing of the innumerable diseases of olden times."

Like any utopia, the world the Vernes describe is a reflection of the values of their own era. In particular it speaks to their faith in the seemingly limitless potential of science and technology. The dream of unprecedented mastery of the natural world and its resources. "Little though they seem to think of it, the people of this twenty-ninth century live continually in fairyland," they write. "Surfeited as they are with marvels, they are indifferent in presence of each new marvel. To them all seems natural."

And yet amidst all this wonder, Fritz Napoleon Smith is lonely. His wife has gone away to Paris, many miles from the new American capital of Centropolis. We are told that this is the first time in a decade of marriage that Mrs. Edith Smith, who the Vernes are at pains to note is a "professional model," has gone away for so long. Desiring to see her, Fritz turns to a device called the phonotelephote.

As soon as he switches the device on, a live image of Mrs Smith appears in the telephote mirror hanging in front of him. It is a fantastical vision, like the magic mirror in "Snow White," except that this is a very modern technological wonder, employing what the Vernes describe as "a series of sensitive mirrors connected by wires" to link Fritz's office in Centropolis to Mrs Smith's bedroom in Paris. One switch flicked and there she is, an apparition from across the ocean, sleeping off the previous night's revelry. "She is asleep, her head sunk in the lace-covered pillows. What? She stirs? Her lips move. She is dreaming, perhaps? Yes, dreaming." Mr Smith sees every movement, every tiny flutter of an eyelid or quiver of a lip, as clear as if she were right there in the room next to him.

It is a throwaway moment in the story. A romantic interlude in the middle of all this grandeur and progress. And yet it is significant. Whilst the mechanism itself may be fanciful, this is perhaps the first known instance in history when a mechanical device has been imagined for the purpose of conveying images instantaneously from one place to another. This is a completely new idea, one conceived in the midst of a period of technological upheaval that was transforming human understanding of space and time. The year 1889 is just twelve years after the invention of the telephone and less than half a decade before the birth of cinema. The Vernes drew these threads together to conceive of a previously unimaginable possibility. It would be an idea that would lodge itself in our collective consciousness for decades to come.

Despite the unfamiliar name and the unlikely mechanism, despite the fact that, for now at least, this machine is being used more for surveillance than conversation, I believe that what we are witness to here is Mr and Mrs Smith conducting the world's first documented video call.

● ● ●

What does the future look like?

Beckie and I have spent the last seven years asking this question. In cities around the world, from Manchester to São Paulo and Auckland to Cairo, we have run workshops with hundreds, maybe even thousands, of primary school children, in which we have asked them to show us what they think the future of their city will look like.

In Lisbon the children imagined a network of pneumatic tubes to shoot people across the city. In Vancouver they designed an underwater restaurant made entirely out of glass so you could watch the fish swim by as you ate. In London they imagined trains covered in plants that sped across the city, sucking carbon dioxide out of the air, and in Madrid they told us about plants big enough to help the elderly walk across the road. But despite the many differences we encountered from place to place, there were two things that every vision of the future contained: flying cars and robots.

These two pieces of technology appear to occupy a special place in the children's imagination. They are like totems, a physical shorthand for a vision of the future in which the world is circumscribed by an array of new technologies, shimmering new marvels that will infiltrate our daily life in every conceivable way.

This techno-utopian vision of the future is one most of us are very familiar with, indeed that most of us to some extent probably share. It is the future we see in the stories of Jules Verne and the writers, artists, cartoonists, filmmakers, and television producers who came after him. Robots will become our obedient servants, cleaning our streets and making our beds. Flying cars will whisk us to work in a matter of seconds and land us back home on our own private landing pad. Artificial intelligence will solve all our problems, bring us closer together, ease the burden of work, provide us with lifelong companions even. All these marvels, embedded so thoroughly into the world of the future that the people that live there no longer appreciate them. They barely even notice them at all.

Once upon a time the video call was another marvellous future technology just like robots and flying cars. Another totem that promised so much about the future.

It wasn't even that long ago. When I was growing up in the 1980s the video call was still something futuristic and fantastical. In the film *Back to the Future Part II*, for example, released in 1989 but set in faraway 2015, where the middle-aged Michael J. Fox is fired by his boss over a video call on the giant flat-screen TV hanging above his fireplace, the words *You're Fired* flashing up on the screen in big white letters. Or in the 1993 film *Demolition Man*, set in 2032, where a sinister Nigel Hawthorne stalks across the floor of an empty grey boardroom, his movements tracked by what looks like a series of futuristic silver parking meters that pivot to face him, revealing as they do so that each contains a human face on a TV screen.

By the end of the twentieth century the video call had been a part of science fiction for over a century. It is there on film as early as 1927, in Fritz Lang's *Metropolis*, but the idea really took hold in the 1960s, when television started to become pervasive, beaming talking pictures into living rooms across the world. From here the possibility of a device that could connect you face to face just as easily seemed tantalisingly close.

When William Hanna and Joseph Barbera launched *The Jetsons* on ABC in 1962, video calling was a central component of the everyday life of the show's family of the future. Although the show only lasted for a year, its twenty-four episodes were rerun so frequently it became an intrinsic part of the future imaginary for generations of children in the US and beyond, going on to be revived in time for my brother and me to watch new episodes as part of our Saturday morning cartoons in the 1980s.

In *The Jetsons*, video calling is everywhere, along with flying cars, robot housemaids, pneumatic transportation tubes, home computers, mobile telephones, and so much more besides. George Jetson's boss uses video calling to keep an eye on him at work and badger him at home; Jane Jetson uses it to check in on her mother and make plans with her friend Gloria; and Judy

Jetson uses it to chat with her boyfriend, grabbing the screen in fright when her dad intrudes on the call. Traffic police use portable videophones in their flying cars to connect with a judge and deliver speedy justice for any traffic violations. Even Rosey the robot uses video chat, her antennae fizzing like sparklers as she gazes through the screen at her robot beloved.

As *The Jetsons* makes clear, this imagined version of the video call, like the flying car and the robot, is so compelling partly because it is so banal. It is not something completely new and inconceivable (like a global network of computers containing the entirety of human knowledge that is accessible from a device that you can carry with you in a bag or your back pocket). It is, rather, a version of what we already have, but different. A car, but one that flies. A server or an assistant or a teacher or a taxi driver, but one that is a machine. A meeting or a conversation, but one that takes place through our television screens. These imagined devices speak of a life that is already comfortingly familiar to us, enhanced by the seemingly benign promise of all this wondrous new technology.

Mr and Mrs Smith, the Jetsons, Marty McFly—watch them all reclining in their comfortable future chairs, sipping their future drinks, eating their future dinners. They are talking into mirrors and computer screens and television sets. The pictures are flawless. The connections perfect. They make it look so easy. For a hundred years they taught us that this was what the future would look like. This is what it would *feel* like. That it would be easy, convenient, maybe even fun. Just like the present, only better.

• • •

At the same time the Jetsons were first plugging in their video-phones, the practical history of video calling was also beginning in earnest. And where could be more perfect for the techno-utopian dreams of the near future to finally be realised than at the New York World's Fair of 1964?

This was, after all, the main point of these gargantuan events. To bind together national myth and corporate aspiration and spin them out into a glittering vision of the future, in the process ushering that very particular vision of the future into reality. As Richard Barbrook describes it, the aim of this particular fair was "to demonstrate that the USA was the leader in everything: consumer goods, democratic politics, show business, modernist architecture, fine art, religious tolerance, domestic living and, above all else, new technology." The 1939 World's Fair, held on the same site in New York's Flushing Meadows, had predicted a future of suburban comfort, with automatic washing machines and dishwashers and a car in every driveway, and by 1964 this vision had become reality for many Americans. The 1964 fair promised even more. It imagined space tourism in the near future, landing ports on future apartment buildings where aeroplanes would take off vertically into the clear blue sky. Electricity so cheap and readily available it didn't need to be metered. IBM promised robots smart enough to serve our every need. Bell Aerospace sent a man in a jet pack soaring into the sky above the elegant white curves of the fair's vast pavilions.

And at their stand, AT&T introduced a new device they called the Picturephone.

The Picturephone was AT&T's attempt at creating the world's first functioning system for true video calling. There had been earlier versions, such as an experimental Bell Labs device in 1927, but that involved only one-way video and needed a room full of equipment to operate. By the time the Picturephone came to market in 1970, AT&T had spent $500 million developing this new device, predicting that it would become a familiar feature in middle-class American households the way so many of the devices at the 1939 World's Fair had already done.

The phone certainly looked like something out of a science fiction film—all moulded plastic and smooth curves. At the front a disarmingly simple oval-shaped panel contained a small rectangular TV screen, a speaker and a little camera lens. All of this was connected to a more familiar telephone handset into which you needed to speak to be heard. The phone at the World's Fair was connected to another Picturephone at Disneyland in California, where it was installed as part of Tomorrowland, Walt Disney's own World's Fair in microcosm, an exhibition of the future built inside the recycled set of the old Jules Verne film *20,000 Leagues Under the Sea*; one future nested inside another like a Russian doll.

In grainy footage from the New York World's Fair you can see the Picturephone in action. The image on the device is surprisingly good. A flickering, monochrome portrait of a woman in thick-framed glasses looking into the camera and waving.

She laughs and her eyes glance away briefly towards something or someone in the room with her, smiling as if to acknowledge to them the wonder of it all. This intimation of the future. A chance to meet with a stranger face to face across the width of a vast continent.

However, as with so much from the 1964 fair, away from the grand pavilions of Flushing Meadows the Picturephone failed to take off. The commercial model released in 1970 garnered only around five hundred subscribers in total. People complained that they were too expensive and too impractical. They also didn't like the idea of being able to be seen when they were talking on the telephone, preferring the comfort of darkness. The familiarity of unknowing.

In 1964 the corporations that powered the space-age ambitions of the World's Fair were overreaching, promising a future they could not deliver and that it wasn't clear the people actually wanted anyway. As Richard Barbrook puts it, "Hyper-reality had collided with reality—and lost." In the coming decades the force of that techno-utopian dream would wane and sour. Those old *Jetsons* episodes were rerun again and again on TV, but the vision of the future they imagined remained resolutely out of reach.

And yet, throughout the turmoil of the 1970s and '80s, in one place in particular, that utopic vision of a technologically augmented future remained defiantly alive. Not that far north of Disneyland, in the area of California that became known as Silicon Valley, the breathless pace of advancements in computing was incubating a whole new digital infrastructure that would finally, a half-century later, appear ready to fulfil the long-delayed promises of the 1960s.

• • •

I am watching a video of Steve Jobs striding across the stage of the Moscone Center in downtown San Francisco, delivering one of his legendary Apple product launches. He is wearing a black polo neck sweater and a pair of blue jeans. The stage is almost completely empty, except for a table and chair off to one side and, hanging right in the middle, a screen the size of the wall of a house.

Jobs has already been on stage for over an hour, slowly whipping the audience into a state of exultation. He is introducing the latest iteration of the company's flagship device—the iPhone. The audience gasp and cheer. Each nugget of information about the product—its size, its weight, the brightness of the display, the range of apps it supports—is treated like the discovery of a new continent or a message beamed back from some distant planet. Like Jules Verne, Jobs is in the business of revelations, glimpses into a future we didn't realise has already arrived. A World's Fair delivered one carefully scripted line at a time.

Jobs walks to the side of his giant empty stage and sits down in a chair. He looks thin and a little frail. It is 2010. He has not yet announced publicly that the cancer he was first diagnosed with in 2003 has returned. In January 2011 he will leave Apple, initially on a medical leave of absence and then permanently in August. He will die only a couple of months later, in October 2011, at the age of 56.

From his chair by the side of the stage, Jobs opens his new iPhone 4 and tells the audience he is going to call Apple's head designer, Jony Ive, reminding the gathering sternly that they should all have logged off the auditorium Wi-Fi before he does so. The audience can see the phone screen projected several feet wide in front of them, and a few whoops and whistles puncture the solemn silence as Jobs makes his call. As the call connects, the first thing the audience see is Jobs's face filling the iPhone screen. He looks expectant, maybe a little nervous. Then a few seconds later his face is joined by that of a smiling Jony Ive, and as this happens the ripple of applause turns into a torrent. Video calling—or FaceTime, as Apple will call it—has arrived on the iPhone and, this crowd are realising, they are the first to bear witness to it.

By this point the concept of video calling is no longer as novel or futuristic as it was in 1964. The online telecommunications company Skype was founded way back in 2003, and by 2010 had 124 million average monthly users trying and mostly failing to find a good connection. The year 2010 is also the year of Chatroulette, an online platform that sparked a short-lived phenomenon by randomly pairing users via a simple video interface, promising the wondrous opportunity to suddenly be face to face with a stranger anywhere in the world, but in reality offering little more than a relentless parade of erect penises displayed with misplaced pride by their anonymous, headless owners. Video calling has definitively emerged out of the digital sludge, becoming part of the furniture of our online lives.

Despite this, FaceTime feels different. Much closer in conception to the simplicity of those early science fiction devices—the ones their creators imagined would be integrated into our lives with frictionless ease. Wherever you are, whatever you are doing, you can simply press a button on your handset and a face appears on the screen.

This event, then, should be a celebration. Another victory lap for Apple and its superstar CEO. The ultimate fulfilment of a century of promises. The future we have all been waiting for. "You know, this is amazing," Jobs says. "I grew up here in the US with *The Jetsons* and with *Star Trek* and communicators, and just dreaming about this, you know, dreaming about video calling, and it's real now." On the word *real*, his voice goes up an octave and his eyes widen, as if he himself cannot believe what his company has achieved.

And yet nothing about this interaction is quite right. There is a disconnect. Jony Ive floats there on the screen, never sure when the right moment to speak is, smiling and staring into the camera with the glazed-over uncertainty of the subject of a hostage video or a Victorian gentleman having his photograph taken for the first time. Jobs is also smiling, but through gritted teeth. His sense of wonder at a childhood dream finally realised undercut by his visible frustration that a lack of bandwidth is creating a slight delay on the call. He playfully, not-really-that-playfully scolds the audience for not disconnecting their devices from the venue's Wi-Fi. "This thing never freezes up," he insists, "so some of you haven't switched off your Wi-Fi. Come on, let's get it off, please."

Even on this hallowed stage, in front of this audience of true believers, it is all just a bit, well, awkward. Ive keeps smiling and tries to play along. "I grew up watching exactly the same TV shows," he says. "I used to love that sort of wonderful, optimistic view of the future, and it's real now, isn't it?"

"It's real," intones Jobs. "Especially when people turn their Wi-Fi stuff off!"

Jobs clearly blames the audience for his and Ive's lack of connection, but watching now, over a decade later, I'm not sure he was right. I don't think the awkwardness of their interaction is caused by the slight lag on the line. It is the fact that they are in two different worlds. Jobs is on his vast stage, in front of a room full of hundreds of people hanging on his every word. He is reaching the climax of an hour of talking, his heart no doubt racing, his voice booming out of the PA system, echoing through that great, cavernous space. Jony Ive is in what looks like a small office. A painting hangs on the wall behind him. This is his one moment—his only job in this entire theatrical production. It's hard to say how many other people are in the room, but it can't be that many, if any at all. He may know in theory how many people are watching Steve Jobs—he himself was probably watching along too—but he cannot *feel* it.

These two old friends are in very different places. It is no surprise that they might feel a separation; the problem comes because they are acting like there isn't one. The whole premise of the device, as Jobs is asking us to imagine it, is that it provides a seamless, frictionless connection, allowing us to really see each other. But it is clear to me that it doesn't. It is an illusion. These two men are nothing more to each other than an abstraction. A pair of faces on a pair of screens.

It should have served as a warning about what was to come.

• • •

By the year 2020, FaceTime had been around for an entire decade, and developments like higher-definition video had made the experience more dynamic whilst 4G connectivity and fibre-optic broadband helped minimise the lag problems that so frustrated Steve Jobs during his launch presentation. Skype now had over a billion and a half registered users, and competing platforms for online video chat were also beginning to emerge. Just the previous year a predominantly business-focused videoconferencing company called Zoom, founded by former Cisco software engineer Eric Yuan, had completed its initial public offering, ending its first day of trading valued at $16 billion.

Then COVID-19 struck, and towns and cities almost everywhere were placed in lockdown—billions of people, for the first time in their lives, unable to go out, visit friends, participate in the everyday encounters that usually made up their day. As a consequence these video platforms quickly became a necessary solution to the problem of our connectivity. Video calling, and Zoom in particular, was our means of maintaining friendships, conducting meetings, teaching classes or lectures, and participating in art events. On December 31, 2019, there were 10 million daily meetings on Zoom. By April 2020 there were 300 million.

For almost everyone trapped inside a lockdown with access to a computer or a smartphone, video calling was no longer a burgeoning facet of our social lives, it *was* our social lives.

There is much that can be learnt from this impromptu experiment in total online social immersion. For example, one thing that became apparent is how easy it is to make our social, professional, and artistic spaces accessible to people from their own homes. If you cannot physically be at an event, it turns out there are straightforward ways you can nonetheless be present, and there is no excuse not to continue to make those options available to people who need them even after the pandemic is over, both to render those events more accessible and potentially save a huge amount of unnecessary travel.

But we also learnt quite quickly that video calling has its problems. In the years before lockdown, most people experienced video calling only in small doses if at all. And for all but the most tech-savvy users, the experience of the medium was still conditioned in part by its novelty—the thrill of faraway faces appearing on the screen in front of us like in a science fiction story. As late as 2019, a *Forbes* article quotes Zoom's own customer service chief, Jim Mercer, describing in wonder his first encounter with the company's video conferencing platform, describing its ability to manage so many video feeds with such seeming ease as being almost like "voodoo."

It was only as this novelty gave way to full pandemic-enforced immersion in video calling—for work, for entertainment, for socialising—that a broader recognition began to emerge of how exhausting these platforms could be. How draining. How frequently awkward, embarrassing, and alienating. The term *Zoom fatigue* was coined for the particular quality of tiredness that too many video calls generated; a heaviness, like battery acid leaking into your brain.

Academics like Jeremy Bailenson, founding director of the Virtual Human Interaction Lab at Stanford University in California, have diagnosed multiple causes of this condition: the absence of the social cues we normally take from people's body language and the increased cognitive load this absence imposed on us in conversation; an excess of sensory stimulation caused by all these close-up faces staring right at each other all the time; the self-consciousness caused by watching ourselves at the same time as we are looking at the person we are supposed to be talking to; the restriction of our movement, constrained by the tiny box our video camera frames for us. In an article in the journal *Technology, Mind, and Behavior*, Bailenson proposes a series of helpful remedies for these problems—some that we can undertake ourselves, such as sitting farther away from the camera and more regularly switching the video feed off, and others that would require redesigns of the video platforms themselves.

The implication seemingly is that all these issues are bugs that can be fixed. That Zoom fatigue is a temporary affliction that can be ironed out in time. Bailenson himself emphasises that he believes the similarities between face-to-face meetings and Zoom meetings far outnumber the differences. "Indeed," he writes, "the success of this medium, like many technologies, revolves around its ability to seamlessly mimic face-to-face conversations."

• • •

The techno-utopians of the past—from Jules Verne to Steve Jobs—promised a world of frictionless technological integration. A world very much like our own, but better—augmented by digital devices that could seamlessly reproduce the kinds of social encounters we were already familiar with. And so, when our social world was taken away from us, we attempted to reproduce it online, using software largely designed by businesspeople *for* businesspeople. We made dinner parties and pub quizzes, birthday parties, classrooms, lecture theatres, into theatres. And we tried to make them work just like the ones we had known before.

Humans are animals whose strongest sense is sight. Looking is what we are usually best at. For that reason the telephone, the device we used to use to connect us over large distances, was always defined by a sense of separation. Unseen by one another, a conversation on the telephone is an encounter defined by darkness, unknowing, often by uncertainty, trepidation, even longing.

In contrast, the visual component of video chat encourages us to believe that the connection we have is somehow more profound. The founding myths of video chat relied upon the assumption that it could function almost like a window, or like Fritz Napoleon Smith's magic telephote mirror. That the medium itself could disappear, enabling the participants to interact as if they were really sharing a space together.

The pandemic taught us that a myth is all that this is. However advanced it may be, the technology is *not* currently seamless. I believe it won't ever be. Not because of a lack of bandwidth or any failure of design or implementation, but simply because the medium itself cannot disappear. The experience of interacting over video chat is profoundly different to a face-to-face conversation. However frictionless the platforms become, they are still platforms, attempting to convince us that we are sharing the same space when in fact we are not. Like Steve Jobs and Jony Ive, we remain in different places, satellites on our own trajectories—in proximity but fundamentally alien to one another. And the more we try to obscure or ignore that, the more awkward our encounters become.

• • •

In truth I think the warnings were there all along about what was coming down the line. Despite the image they projected of our radiant future, those early science fiction stories also contained, perhaps unintentionally, intimations of the discomfort, the weirdness, the alienation that would accompany their eventual arrival.

They were there in an uncomfortable half-argument that Mr Fritz Napoleon Smith and Mrs Edith Smith have when they sit down together at the telephote in 2889, convincing themselves it was possible to share a meal but realising too late that it might have been breakfast time for Mr Smith, but Mrs Smith's day had begun many hours previously—he was left waiting impatiently whilst she was already up and out and in the world. They were there also in *The Jetsons*, when Jane Jetson, on receiving a call unexpectedly from her friend Gloria, hurriedly puts on a mask of her own face rather than letting Gloria see her without any make-up on, only to realise half-way through the call that Gloria has done exactly the same thing. Two masked women staring uncomfortably at each other from behind their disguises, making plans as if nothing is amiss, like everything is completely normal.

But it's not normal. It's awkward. It's strange. They are smiling fondly at one another, pretending they are breathing in the same air. Convincing themselves they can feel the solid ground beneath their feet, when really they are floating in space.

● ● ●

What can we do then? Is all hope for the future lost?

I think the answer might lie in a civil forfeiture hearing in Texas's 394th Judicial District Court which accidentally became the best thing that happened on the internet in 2021. Attorney Rod Ponton had borrowed his assistant's laptop to log into the hearing, which was taking place over Zoom, not knowing that last time she used it she had apparently been playing with Zoom's filter feature, which enabled the user to overlay their own face with that of someone or something else.

So, when Ponton switched on his video, rather than his own face becoming visible, his voice appeared to be coming from a fluffy grey kitten whose sad blue eyes stared confusedly into the camera.

"Mr Ponton, I believe you have a filter turned on in the video settings," the judge in the case politely told him. Ponton blinked his big cat eyes and explained in a faintly agonised voice that his assistant was trying to remove the filter but didn't know how to. He assured the rest of the hearing that he was prepared to go forward with it, if they were, before adding: "I'm here live. I'm not a cat." At which point, finally, everyone in the Zoom room began to smile.

There is something so wonderful about this video. I could watch it every day and never get bored of it. The formality of the court. The soulfulness of the cat. The collision of the real and unreal, the serious and the unserious. The medium shimmering, revealing itself, and the strangeness of our shared relationship to it—all these people sat in front of their laptops, trying their hardest to conduct an actual real-world meeting in a digital space of instability and illusion.

Zoom first introduced filters in August 2020, in large part in response to all the reports of Zoom fatigue. They were, in the company's own words, an attempt to enable people "to feel your best in virtual meetings, express your individuality, and build moments of fun into your day." More importantly, however, these filters draw attention to Zoom itself—to the interface that mediates our interactions with one another. They help us to render visible the otherness of a video call. By pointing to its artifice, they invite us to explore the possibilities this artificial space permits. Possibilities that no longer need to be constrained by the need to replicate how people interact in the real world.

What might video calling become once we recognise it isn't what the stories of the past told us it would be? How can we begin to learn the contours of this entirely new form of encounter?

I think the answer lies in part in acknowledging, even celebrating, the thing that we have previously tried to diminish—the disconnection, that otherness, our inherent separation from one another. Maybe all our meetings should be conducted as cats, or maybe we should point our cameras out the window rather than at our own faces—a collage of views, contradictory perspectives, different shades of sky. Let's find ways to be playful, and by doing so hopefully insert compassion into digital spaces that have been far too denuded of it.

In February 2021, Beckie and I were working with a group of teenagers in São Paulo, logging onto Zoom each evening from our small apartment in London to make a theatre show with them from their bedrooms in Brazil. As part of our attempts to overcome the inherent awkwardness of this virtual rehearsal room, we'd start every session with a different game, each an attempt not just to bring us closer together but also to recognise and play around with our separation from one another. One day we asked them to find something in their house that made them happy and bring it back to the computer. Another day they each had to describe two objects—one they could see in their room and one that was entirely made up—and then the rest of us had to guess which was which.

But perhaps the most popular game of all was one we ended up calling Rainbow Screen. Everyone in the call was assigned a different colour, and then told to switch their video off and spend five minutes filling their screen with as much of that colour as possible—stuffed toys, ornaments, clothes, books, random swatches of fabric, whatever you could lay your hands on. After the five minutes, we all switched our video back on simultaneously.

As we did so the screen lit up like a firework. Each individual window was its own private monochromatic rectangle, a world unto itself. But when seen together through Zoom's matrix of video squares they became something else entirely—a new universe, neither real nor unreal, existing in no one particular place. A digital rainbow. An unearthly riot of colour.

CHAPTER 4

A HOME YOU CAN CARRY
WITH YOU

There will come a time—there must surely come a time—in the far distant future when cars are a thing of the past and no living person remembers what it was like to drive in one. When all the roads have been dug up or grown over. When the remains of elevated skyways crumble like Grecian ruins and the discovery of a battered licence plate in some great-grandfather's attic draws nothing but blank stares. When the only remaining cars are skeletons in museums, or images in films and photographs, or tiny scale models of twentieth-century cities with thousands upon thousands of miniature cars moving in endless, hypnotic circles.

When this time comes, what will the people of the future make of this peculiar invention? What will they think about us and all the things these vehicles meant to us? How will they ever understand? How will they make sense of our endless affection for these doomed appliances? The way in movies we treated them with such reverence, such affection, such hunger. How we named them and cleaned them, polished them to a shine. Will they gaze in bafflement at picture after picture of shiny new cars displayed like works of art in showrooms and conference centres? At all the adverts where cars move like dreams through twilit cities and sun-drenched mountain passes?

They will try and try to understand, but in truth they never really will. To them the car will be nothing but an object. A historical fact. An engineering marvel that blazed so brightly for a couple of hundred years, leaving the world scorched and overheated in its wake.

• • •

In 2010 I was invited by a theatre in Glasgow to create a new show for a special season of events happening whilst their building was closed for renovations. Propose anything you want, they said, as long as it doesn't require a theatre. After some pondering I told them I wanted to make a show that could happen inside a car parked on the roof of a nearby multi-storey car park, and that in order to do so I would need the theatre to buy me a car. To my surprise they actually did. They paid £200 for a secondhand white Suzuki Swift bought from my friend Gemma. The first car I had ever owned. It looked like a bad drawing of a car and shook nervously whenever it went over fifty miles per hour, but I loved it completely till the day it died.

The show I made with this car was an attempt to understand our strange and ill-fated relationship with the automobile.

I imagined my car as a museum exhibit thousands of years in the future. A means for the people of that time to learn about the people of our time. Playing the role of these citizens of the future, pairs of audience members wearing headphones sat in the back seat of the Suzuki Swift and a voice in their ears began to tell them stories. The engine purred and the radio whispered and they ventured off on their imagined journey. They were part of a family setting out across a desert highway, then they were two horny teenagers parked up at a drive-in movie theatre, then a taxi driver and a passenger stuck in traffic in the pouring rain.

The show attempted to collapse the mythic and the mundane into one another. It glittered with fabulous images of faraway places and the music was forever soaring, but all the while the two audience members were sitting all alone in the back seat of a £200 hatchback on the roof of a rainy Glasgow car park.

The more the show was performed—up and down the motorways of the UK, on the roof of another multi-storey car park in Bristol, inside an old military drill hall in Edinburgh, in a muddy field on the edge of a forest at a musical festival in Suffolk, in a former meat market in Madrid—the more apparent it became to me that a large part of the fondness that we somehow retain for these dangerous contraptions had nothing at all to do with driving them. It was instead to do with the encounters we are able to have in them.

Sure, some people love them for the speed or the mechanics. Some love them as markers of their own prosperity. But none of this love is what I saw in the show. What I saw was two people lost together inside a world they were busy creating for themselves; following the instructions on their headphones, giggling together as they played at driving, or parking up in some quiet spot, or just sleeping with their foreheads resting on the cool window. Often passers-by would stop to inquire what was going on, gaping confusedly as the audience members opened car doors and slammed them shut again or sat together in the front seat, arms draped over each other's shoulders, gazing out at precisely nothing. But no amount of staring from any onlookers was enough to distract the audience members inside.

Behind the reinforced glass, the windows wound right up, they were in their own private universe, sharing in an experience that belonged exclusively to them. Enjoying an encounter of profound intimacy that forever teetered on the border between public and private. Between in here and out there.

Act 1

Picture yourself there. Headphones on, lying on the back seat, head leaning against the cold glass of the car window, staring up at a sliver of sky. Underneath you, the murmur of the engine cradles you in its arms. You breathe slowly, feeling that gentle tug as the car moves this way and that. Above you, you glimpse street lights, motel signs, the corner of a building, passing clouds. You could be on holiday, driving through exotic-sounding places with names like Cortina Allegro Sierra Fiesta Montego Cordoba Pacifica Mondeo Sunbeam, or you could just be on your way to the shops again, or to Grandma's, or there could be no purpose to this journey at all other than to get you to fall asleep. If so, then it's working. Your eyes are sliding closed, and soon you will be fast asleep.

• • •

When I was very young my mum's one reliable method for getting me to go to sleep was to strap me into the passenger seat of her little white Mini and just drive around for a while. Any time of the day or night, it was guaranteed to work. It was like a magic trick; almost as soon as she had started the engine I was drifting away. I do not remember any of these encounters but I'm sure she does, attempting to concentrate on the road whilst this tiny person lay sleeping just out of reach.

It would appear this technique was one of those little pieces of advice passed from parent to parent in the pre-internet age. A shared secret with a remarkable success rate. A 2012 survey by the UK retailer Mothercare found that over half of the thousand parents they spoke to would regularly use the car as a way to get their child to fall asleep. There are, no doubt, thousands of them out there right now, those exhausted parents and their sleeping children, driving around in endless circles. Making neat circuits of their neighbourhood in the sunshine. Promenading up and down empty stretches of motorway in the early hours of the morning. Passing the same billboard for the thousandth time, listening to late-night love songs on the radio, looking over occasionally to check on their sleeping passengers.

What is it about a car in motion that brings babies such comfort? Some developmental psychologists have pointed to the ways in which the experience of constant low-level movement and the muffled white noise of the engine might evoke in very young children the memory of being in the womb, gently drawing us back to that earliest tranquillity. A metal cocoon to replace the one in which we grew and slept for so long, and from which we were so recently and traumatically ejected.

It is strange to think that from such a young age, so many people could come to associate a machine as dangerous as a car with a feeling of comfort and protection—the site of some of our earliest and most tender encounters. In the US, cars kill almost as many people each year as guns do. And yet there is something about that little metal bubble. The privacy and the warmth. The way we can wrap it around ourselves like a blanket or a spacesuit. A barrier that can protect us from the riotous strangeness of the world without ever obscuring it entirely.

As we get older, I think we carry the memory of those encounters with us. That engine hum working like a Valium even after we stop associating this box of machinery with the serenity of the womb. Instead, with its thick windows, its lockable doors, and its consumer electronics, the car becomes an extension of the comfort and security of the home. An extra room on wheels. A little corner of domestic life we can break off and carry with us on our travels.

My family would drive everywhere together, listening to the same cassette tapes over and over, reading books until we felt sick, playing car games—counting the red cars and the white cars—arguing about nothing until my brother and I fell asleep. These trips are burnt into my memory, spooling together into one single, unending journey down all the motorways of the UK, stopping at every service station on the way. An odyssey of melted chocolate and toilet stops. A family road trip that was as long, as fun, as boring, as infuriating, and as joyful as my childhood itself.

The whole idea of a family car relies upon some assumptions about the size of a family that did not become consolidated in the US and Europe until around the same time as the automobile was being invented. Motor vehicles big enough for and marketed towards the family began appearing as early as the 1920s, just as cars began to be thought of as a middle-class appliance rather than simply an upper-class plaything. Estate cars (or station wagons) were manufactured using versions of existing vehicles such as the Model A Ford, modified to accommodate a larger number of passengers and a greater volume of luggage. Originally intended for military and commercial purposes, they were also nonetheless advertised to the general public, where their popularity quickly soared.

However, the version of the family that these cars could accommodate was strictly limited. There was no room for a whole extended family—aunts, uncles, grandparents, and the like. Then and now, a family car tended to be the ideal size for two parents, their children, and perhaps one or two other adults at most. As such, these vehicles helped normalise a particular definition of what constitutes a single ordinary family. A "nuclear family," the term itself popularised around the same time as these family cars began flying off the production line.

Something was happening here; inside this moving metal box, a way of thinking about yourself and your relationship with the people around you was taking shape. In many ways the car is the perfect articulation of the values traditionally associated with the nuclear family. Autonomous, private, self-contained. Even the way the seats are laid out helps reinscribe a particular blueprint for how the conventional family should operate—father in the driver's seat, mother next to him, and the children in the back. This model is disappointingly persistent—a 2010 study by the Institute of Advanced Motorists found that when heterosexual partners are in the car together, the male partner is four times more likely to be the driver than the female, and that those women drivers are much more likely to feel uncomfortable when driving their male partner.

Together the nuclear family can drive wherever they want to go, present in the world but set apart from it, looking out at the passing fields, the buildings, the other cars, seeing it all from behind cold glass, like a safari park or a movie made just for them. The family becomes the lens through which each individual engages with and experiences their surrounding environment, to the detriment of the kind of outside influences a person will inevitably encounter when they are not encased in metal and travelling at forty miles an hour. There is none of the noise and mess of the city streets here, just a nucleus of people spinning in their own private orbit.

How does this introduction to the world influence the way we perceive the things and people around us? Has the detachment of the family car influenced the outsized role that the nuclear family has come to assume within Western society? Have these devious machines taught us that family should always come first?

What is certainly true is that within the limited space of the family car, the social and civic bonds that might have once connected us to some larger whole are in danger of being squeezed out, caught like some errant finger in a slamming metal door.

On our back seat my brother and I would turn away from the world outside to pull faces at each other, turning back when my mum would point out a field of sheep or a passing sports car or a glimpse of the twinkling sea appearing finally on the horizon. When it rained, the windscreen wipers would thrum like a heartbeat, and we could watch pedestrians running for cover. We traced the paths of raindrops streaming across the windows whilst inside we remained completely dry.

Act 2

When you open your eyes again, things have changed. You are in the front seat now. A little bit older, a little bit wiser. You are parked in a quiet spot—it could be a rest stop just off the motorway, or a parking space under a poorly lit railway arch. It could be high up at some lover's lookout, overlooking the constellation of lights illuminating the town below. In the darkness, the interior of the car is nothing but shadows and space, the only light coming from the dashboard, which glows red and green and orange. Despite this you can feel the presence of someone beside you, see their chest rising and falling in time with your own. The radio plays a series of intimate pop classics, each more outlandishly suggestive than the last—"Born to Be Wild," "Shut Up and Drive," "Into My Arms," "Physical," "Let's Get It On," "Crash," "Dream Baby Dream." You feel yourselves bound together, encased in suggestively moulded plastic and imitation leather. Interlocking gears in some relentless mechanism. Lovers in a film about young lovers who drive around together, being in love, illuminated by the internal glow of their electric hearts.

• • •

Since almost the very beginning, cars have been sold on the promise of freedom.

Cars, we have always been told, enable us to go anywhere and do anything. As early as 1924, Ford advertisements were seducing prospective buyers with the idea that "To own a Ford car is to be free to venture into new and untried places," and even today car commercials continue to be preoccupied with the spectre of exploration and adventure. Oversized SUVs ripping through some desert valley, kicking up great plumes of dust in their wakes. An elegant sedan mastering the bends of an empty forest road. A bright red convertible disappearing into the sunset. Discovery. Escape. Going farther. Going through. Going beyond.

But there is more than one kind of freedom. Most of us will likely never plunge through a mountain pass in an over-priced Subaru or attempt to traverse the Mediterranean in some tumble-down Volkswagen camper. Not every car is a means of escape to new and untried places. For many people a car is a destination in itself. A place of encounter and intimacy, of friendship and joy and, yes, freedom. Perhaps their only such place.

For teenagers and young adults in particular, especially those still living at home and sharing rooms with brothers and sisters, privacy is a scarce commodity. No space truly your own. When you live in someone else's house, you live by their rules. But if you can scrimp and save to get yourself a car, you can change all of that. You can set your own rules. You can mark out these few cubic metres of air for you and you alone. The possessor of that thing so seemingly integral to the Western psyche: private property.

And you can choose the colour and the make. You can pick out the seats and paint a stripe on the side. You can litter it with tacky ornaments or nudie pictures. Dangle prayer beads or family photos or a scented Christmas tree from the rearview mirror. You can allow it to become littered with cigarette butts and burger wrappers, let mud lick its way up the side in the hope the rain will wash it off. Or you can keep it spotlessly clean and polished to a shine. You choose the music. You choose the sound system. Install a subwoofer that rattles the walls of passing houses. Tint the windows. Stick strips of blue neon to the undercarriage. Cover the back seat in changes of clothes, dog toys, magazines. Fill the glove compartment with sand if you want. This place belongs entirely to you.

For generations now, young people have been figuring themselves out inside these curious metal pods, free from the rules and expectations they are beholden to at home. Gathering with friends and lovers, talking, smoking, drinking, having fun.

In many ways a car is a perfect place to do these things—a spatial architecture that might have been designed to facilitate encounters of close proximity amongst nervous young people whilst avoiding much of the awkwardness that might otherwise ensue.

An encounter in a car is like a beginners class in conversation. The arrangement of the seats minimises the need for eye contact, which researchers have shown can be actively inhibiting when trying to form new thoughts, whilst at the same time the combination of the stereo and the world outside provide comforting background noise and a limitless store of distractions. A car is in many ways the ideal environment in which to tentatively begin to explore new ways of interacting with the people around you.

And then there are the romantic encounters in automobiles that happen at lover's lookouts, in rest stops, and on quiet cul-de-sacs, or right out in the open, depending on how brazen you are feeling. I will never forget the time I stumbled upon what I have to assume was two people having sex in a parked car in the middle of the night in Edinburgh city centre. The vehicle rocking up and down with the windows all misted up, the soft moonlight and the otherwise empty university car park burnishing the whole scene with a kind of melancholy grandeur, like an X-rated Edward Hopper painting.

The relationship between sex and cars is long and fraught, the two irresistibly drawn to each other. Hands pressed against fogged-up windows, awkward fumblings in too-small back seats. Is a car actually ever that sexy? I would argue that it is not. But where else can young people meet to have sex, especially in less permissive environments? The closest thing that many people have to a lockable bedroom, the car is a space of privacy and intimacy, just about insulated enough from the rules or expectations that govern our conduct at home or in public space.

Drinking, talking, smoking, fucking—driving too fast down unfamiliar roads and parking in dark corners where you hope no one can see you. All of this is unsafe, in more ways than one, but perhaps the danger is part of the allure. Teetering on the edge of control, of learning maybe for the first time that your actions can have serious consequences, that people can get really hurt. In a car, that precariousness is made tangible—the brittleness of our bones and the softness of our flesh as they rattle around and against one another in this solid metal cage. Learning to drive has become integral to coming of age—a practical test elevated to the status of a symbolic ritual. A becoming into the adult world of danger and sex and responsibility.

I learnt so much about myself as teenager and a young adult in these vehicles. Forged friendships, romances—encounters I will remember forever. All the evenings we spent parked up on the street outside my parents' house. The time we skidded drunkenly round an empty field on the edge of our friend's farm. The night we drove home from Swansea in the rain, chain-smoking Marlboro reds like we thought we were cowboys. All the moments when I was learning to understand myself and my relationships with the people I cared about most in these hurtling boxes of gasoline and glass and electronics.

Act 3

In our final act we are no longer together. You are in the front seat and I am in the back, or maybe it's the other way around. To me you are just a pair of eyes floating in the rearview mirror. Around us there is nothing but other cars. Lanes and lanes of static traffic, red tail-lights catching the exhaust fumes as they spiral upwards. Shadowy figures loom in the murky interiors but you can't make them out. Traffic lights flick uselessly between colours, but no one pays them any attention. We aren't really speaking. Two strangers now in our own separate worlds. It's dark outside, but for some reason you cannot remember if it's really early or really late. The cars inch forward and you stare out of the window, listening to the chorus of car horns and drifting slowly off to sleep.

• • •

Cars tend to lose their sparkle as we get older. Another part of life, like going into town or receiving a letter in the post, that is slowly worn down by repetition and the responsibilities of adulthood. What was once a new space of exploration and self-discovery becomes part of the cycle of work life, familial obligation, and the necessary maintenance required to keep ourselves and our loved ones in the world.

In general I think the most interesting encounters that adults tend to have in cars are not with loved ones—people they have most likely grown comfortably familiar with—but are rather those short and transactional interactions that occur between strangers when one person is responsible for driving the other to their destination. An encounter between a taxi driver and a customer: two people completely unknown to one another confined temporarily in close proximity. Here the much-discussed intimacy of a car takes on a completely different quality. How do these people choose to interact when thrown together inside this intimate bubble? Do they talk? Do they argue? Do they meet each other's gaze? Do they even acknowledge one another beyond the requirement to say where it is that the passenger wishes to go? Such encounters involve a series of decisions by both parties that usually slowly build some kind of fragile trust—enough of a connection to sustain them over the course of their shared journey.

Where, for example, should you sit in a taxi? In most places the convention is that the passenger sits in the back. In cities like London and New York there is even a plastic shield that separates the driver's space from the area available to passengers. Sitting in the back of a taxi is a way of rendering visible the separation between the driver and the passenger. It makes clear their fundamental difference, one a service provider and the other a customer, but also in the process highlights the myriad other separations—of class, geography, language—that might exist between them. Talking across this divide is difficult and so not expected. Driver and passenger can float along, together and apart, each in their own parallel reality.

In some places, however, such as Australia and New Zealand and the more rural parts of Scotland and Ireland, the convention is the opposite. The passenger is expected to sit in the front and navigate their encounter without the comfort of distance. And then there are those audaciously bold people who actively choose to sit in the front even when the expectation is that they sit in the back. Such an action is a performance of sorts, an attempt to physically overcome the things that separate you—to locate oneself, literally and figurately, as the driver's equivalent, whether the driver desires this or not.

Here, as in all such unexpected encounters with strangers, there is the potential for beauty and joy, albeit undergirded by the spectre of violence and fear. According to the National Institute for Occupational Health and Safety, taxi drivers have the highest homicide rate of any occupation in the US. They are at least twenty times more likely to be murdered on the job than the average worker, and are the victims of more violent assaults than anyone other than police officers and security guards. In a recent survey by the UK's *i* newspaper, 93 per cent of the drivers admitted suffering racial abuse, some as regularly as every day. Passengers, too, particularly women and marginalised people, enter a taxi or a ride-sharing car with a heightened sensitivity to the inherent risk of harassment and violence that comes from agreeing to be temporarily confined in this way with a complete stranger.

A taxi is a space where notions of public and private are complicated. Where the experience of unpredictability, difference, and occasional hostility that we normally associate with being out in the public realm is confined to a private vehicle. Any encounter in this space is trying to navigate these tensions—the awkwardness of unfamiliarity, the quiet undercurrent of fear. And just like all those teenagers in their cars, we can lean on the vehicle's architecture to help guide us through the awkwardness. Perhaps we can use these interactions as a way to relearn how to navigate the discomfort of encountering strangers. There is something both compassionate and hopeful about our fumbling attempts to acknowledge our differences and find ways of connecting anyway. There is a particular happiness to be found in taking the front seat for once, or just putting your phone away and striking up a conversation, however much you may not want to.

• • •

In the far distant future it will be recorded that the year 2020 was a banner year for the automobile. In the whole sweeping history of the motor vehicle, it never again got any better than this.

On the eve of its obsolescence the car made a temporary comeback as a means of navigating the dangers of a global pandemic. Suddenly a whole slew of activities that people normally did together were now participated in from the comfort and security of their individual cars. In North Somerset in the UK, cars queued patiently to attend drive-through doctor's appointments, whilst in California Snoop Dogg performed to an audience of neatly parked cars at the Ventura County Fairgrounds. There were drive-in stand-up comedy shows, drive-in musicals, drive-through vaccination centres, and drive-through supermarkets. People queued for hours to load their cars up with toilet paper, and in the dusky sunshine of a summer evening I attended my first-ever drive-in movie, watching *Jaws* on a big screen in a car park outside Alexandra Palace.

For these much-maligned vehicles it was like a return to the glory days of the 1950s, when it was drive-in everything and the future belonged to the automobile. It was undoubtedly a strange and somewhat sterile spectacle to see cars arranged neatly in rows, enjoying the kinds of experiences that in other times would bring strangers together to worship or party or laugh or some combination of all three. Whilst I enjoyed the novelty of our drive-in cinema experience, I wouldn't want it to replace the cinema that I love so much. The joyous communality, the gasps and the laughter, and the moments when another world seemed to materialise in the air between us. More than anything the experience of the drive-in made me realise how much of our world we have already given up to cars. The extent to which our lives are already lived in some vast drive-in.

In this terrible plague year, cars provided a barrier between us and the outside world. And they gave us the facsimile of a communal experience, an almost-feeling of breathing the same air, of being together again. But such experiences were also a reminder that this metal carapace, this barrier between us and the world, keeps more than COVID out. As anyone who has ever seen a blurry paparazzi photo of a celebrity attempting to leave their own driveway will know, having any meaningful sense of who is inside is very difficult. In the rain or at night, the actual people inside a car are essentially invisible, lost in a dazzlement of reflective glare.

Our only real way of encountering each other car to car is by employing an arcane language of beeps and flashes as a way to communicate. But these languages are almost entirely contextual, reliant on a shaky presumption of shared understanding. In Egypt, for example, as my friend Shaza once informed me as we navigated a dense current of Cairo traffic, your car horn is everything. It is your indicator and your warning lights, your hello, your thank you, and your fuck off. A device of infinite musical possibility, as the dawn chorus on any busy Cairo street will tell you.

Such ambiguity of intention, coupled with your anonymity within your enclosed vehicle, leads almost inevitably to frequent incidents of road rage. As roads have become more congested, fraught encounters between drivers have increased exponentially, leading to incidents of aggressive driving that have escalated into violence and occasionally even led to serious injury and death. According to the *New York Times*, between 2014 and

2016, a total of 136 people in the US were shot and killed in road rage incidents. Hidden away from each other, swaddled in their anonymity, held together only by the thinnest thread of a communication, car users suffer a breakdown of their sense of shared humanity.

As the car has become the predominant mode of transport in much of the world over the last hundred years, our towns and cities have been transformed to accommodate them. Now roads full of fast-moving cars fracture our communal spaces, dividing neighbourhoods, separating one side of the street from the other, forcing pedestrians to navigate around them. And even when they aren't moving, parked cars occupy huge amounts of space, lined up bumper to bumper along each side of the road, rendering that space unusable by anybody and anything else. A recent study estimated that in London alone, on-street parking takes up over fourteen square kilometres of space, or the equivalent of ten Hyde Parks. All this makes walking and cycling inhospitable, further reducing the amount of time we spend out of our cars. What this all amounts to is essentially a privatisation by stealth of much of our public realm, profoundly changing how we encounter strangers out in the world.

Our increasing reliance on cars has significantly narrowed the opportunities we have to meet and encounter one another. The most profound interactions a person has whilst driving involve a very limited circle of people—family, friends, lovers, the occasional brief journey with a stranger. What, then, of all the other people we pass every day? The people driving beside and around us, immersed in their own little pockets of private space. What capacity do we have to see each other, to interact, to connect with one another? What space is there left for us to encounter each other at all?

We are reaching a point of reckoning. The twentieth century is over and the great romance between humans and automobiles that so illuminated and transformed it is coming to an end. Recently I listened to one of the country's leading air pollution experts tell a group of ten-year-olds that the one clear and obvious thing people could do to reduce air pollution is to stop driving. Will those children ever have the same relationship to a car as I do? Undoubtedly not. They dream of a world without cars. They dream of jet packs and moving floors and streets made of trampolines. They dream of canals and bike lanes and cycle-buses. They dream of pneumatic tubes and tube slides and myriad other solutions to the problem of movement that don't involve us being isolated in these tiny metal boxes.

What is it that we dream of? I dream of childhood road trips and teenage trysts, of late-night taxi rides into the unknown. But I also dream of a time when all of this is forgotten. When the needs and desires these encounters responded to can be satisfied in other ways. I dream of new categories of encounter; new, more equitable relationships between public and private space.

I dream of a time when all these automobiles are so many museum exhibits, looked on with curiosity and despair by people who will never understand why we loved cars so much even as they were always trying to kill us.

CHAPTER 5

SOCIETY IN SIX MEALS

Meal 1: Five Domino's Pizzas

Eslam's dad hand-delivered the pizzas in the back of his taxi and we ate them sitting cross-legged in a circle on the polished wood floor of the theatre's biggest rehearsal room. Cardboard boxes stacked in the centre like a campfire. There were thirteen of us. Me, Beckie, our assistant, Constantina, and the ten primary school children we had been making a show with for the last three weeks.

The show was due to begin in an hour's time. The audience had already started arriving. Beckie, Constantina, and I were all exhausted, and so were the children. All day we had been telling them what to do, asking them to be quiet, acting, to all intents and purposes, like teachers or parents. But takeaway pizza makes certain demands of the people eating it. It demands mucky hands and greasy chins. A temporary abandonment of the politics of manners. The moment the pizza boxes were opened and the smell of baked bread and melted cheese filled the air like fireworks, the hierarchy that usually defined our relationship to each other was temporarily suspended. We talked and laughed together, discussed our favourite pizza toppings, our plans for the summer holidays, our hopes for the future, enjoying a few moments of togetherness stolen back from the busyness of the day. In a few minutes we would all run downstairs—there were costumes to be hustled into, final sound checks to be done, nerves to be calmed, and then the doors would open and the auditorium would start to fill. But all of that was still in the future. For now, we were eating takeaway pizzas together straight from the box, washing them down with plastic cups full of Diet Coca-Cola.

Like a lot of the best foods, pizza was born of a familiar combination of destitution and resourcefulness. On the crowded streets of Naples, an underclass known as the *lazzaroni* struggled to survive, working when they could as porters or messengers, stealing and begging when there appeared to be no other option. Each day these people woke up and attempted to answer an ageless question: How am I going to eat enough to survive for another day? Not an easy question to answer if you have virtually no money to buy food and no kitchen to cook in. The *lazzaroni*'s clever solution was a flat disc of bread topped with tomatoes and herbs. A food so simple it could be made by almost anyone in even the smallest and most cramped kitchens using cheap and readily available ingredients, then eaten by hand out on the city streets.

In Naples, the world's first pizzas were cooked in side-alley kitchens and then cut up into individual slices to be sold to the desperate and the exhausted. Young boys would be hired to zig-zag through the crowded streets displaying their slices of pizza on movable tables. At night, others would carry them on trays past the steps of the apartment buildings where all the old women would sit and rest. For no more than a few pennies they could buy themselves a slice of pizza and eat it where they sat, listening to the noise of the city as it moved ceaselessly around them.

You don't need me to tell you this, but pizza is everywhere now. What began as a food of the poor and hungry Neapolitan masses is now served in white-tiled bistros, garish chain restaurants, and every single hipster bar in the known universe. But although as a food it has changed much in that time—becoming bigger, richer, more expensive—I think it still retains at least some of that originary flavour. It is still, often, a food for the weary. A food of snatched moments. Of impromptu group lunches, exhausted end-of-the-day dinners, and desperate late-night last resorts. Less a meal and more a solution to a problem.

Back when I was nineteen, I would spend nearly every hour I had in a beloved little student theatre in the centre of Edinburgh, a barely converted old church with a little rectangular stage and a hundred red cinema seats squeezed in where the pews once were. Here we would rehearse for hours on end, evenings and weekends, whole days when we were able to, neglecting our actual schoolwork to commit everything we had to productions of grand ambition and variable quality. We performed a rare Rainer Werner Fassbinder play about the Moors Murders and a Howard Barker play about Charles II. For one show we built an artificial hill covered in real turf, whilst for another we adapted the York Mystery Plays into a four-hour long piece of experimental theatre.

This last one I remember particularly well. We rehearsed, appropriately enough, over the Easter holidays whilst everyone else was home with their parents, spending endless hours repainting the entire theatre white, indulging in extended improvisations meant to simulate the Last Supper, turning the betrayal in the Garden of Gethsemane into a tango between Jesus and Judas, and at the end of the day, when no one wanted to go home, we would send someone out to get cheap bottles of red wine from the off-licence over the road and a stack of Domino's pizzas we would eat straight out of the boxes on the bare white stage, paint-flecked and tired-eyed, in love with ourselves and the private universe we had created.

These impromptu meals are some of the fondest memories I have of my entire university life. They were meals of belonging. They spoke of a shared bond—a sense of collective endeavour, however trivial or niche that endeavour might have been. A food from the thronged streets of Naples bringing us together in this cold, deconsecrated church at the other end of this weird continent.

Every meal tells a story about the people sharing it. It is a performance through which we rehearse our relationships to each other. "Of all the things that people have in common," the philosopher Georg Simmel writes in his 1910 essay "The Sociology of the Meal," "the most common is that they must eat and drink." This is a need we all share, and when we eat together—when we share a meal—we recognise that commonality. However different our tastes and our lives may be, we are united in the act of eating and the fundamental purpose it has for us. And yet, at the same time, there is a very real limit on our capacity to share a meal together. Whilst a meal as a whole can be shared, each individual morsel—whether it be a spoonful of soup, a single chocolate, or a segment of orange—can be eaten by only one person, and "what the individual eats," Simmel claims, "no one else can eat under any circumstances." Once we have taken a bite and swallowed it down, that food is inside of us and only us, a thing which must be ours alone.

Sharing a meal with someone is a reminder both of how much we have in common and that we are individual beings fundamentally distinct from one another. A demonstration of the shared bonds that tie us to one another and the bodily autonomy that will always mark the limit of those bonds. No other encounter more succinctly demonstrates the essential nature of our social existence—to be forever negotiating the relationship between ourselves as individuals and the larger communities and societies that we live as part of.

It is perhaps no surprise, then, that eating together has almost always been about more than simple nutrition. Sharing food is a social ritual with a million different histories—too many even for one book, let alone a single essay. When we eat together we reproduce the social world we are a part of, reiterating or even reimagining the terms of our relationships with the people around us. Our shared meals can be a way of showing affection or kinship. They can be a demonstration of our sophistication or our status or our wealth. They can be a kind of entertainment, or a fantasy of the life we want to live and the people we want to share it with. Even the simplest everyday meals are freighted with this kind of symbolic significance—consolidating or disrupting our relationships with the people we are eating with (not to mention the people who weren't invited).

Such significance was present in every one of the hastily assembled takeaway meals we ate in that dusty old theatre-church in Edinburgh, however informal they might have been. "When people share meals," the sociologist Alice Julier writes, "they rely on social knowledge about what to do and how to do it." Our understanding of these "cultural templates" is a way of demonstrating that we share the same values, that we all belong. Such a performance might be more obvious in the complex pantomime of a formal dinner—knowing how to dress appropriately, choosing the right cutlery for each course, not putting your elbows on the table—but five Domino's pizzas cut into slices and eaten straight from their cardboard boxes is still a performance of manners and conventions. It is a dance you either do or don't feel comfortable performing.

Beckie, Constantina, our young collaborators, and I clearly

knew this dance well. We ate with our bare hands slices of pizza torn away from the communal stack, the crumbs falling on the floor and on ourselves, ribbons of rubbery yellow cheese smacking against our chins as we wiped our greasy hands on crumpled paper napkins or the backs of our trousers. The privileged classes of Naples used to think of pizza eaters as revolting, entirely lacking in manners. But this supposed lack of decorum is also another kind of code. A marker of collective debasement. Elite disgust helping to reify the group. Even today there is an intimacy to eating with this kind of informality. The trust and camaraderie that are shared along with the pizza. All those mucky hands serving as their own source of solidarity.

Which is not to say that such meals can't at the same time be a source of private anxiety and insecurity, as meals so often are. Have I got my fair share? Am I eating too much? Can I really afford to be a part of this impromptu feast? Can I pay for just the slices I eat? Why did they order mushrooms when they know I don't like mushrooms? Why are there so many meat pizzas when half of us are vegetarians? How harshly will people judge me if I eat their leftover crusts? Is it OK that I don't actually like pizza all that much?

The individual and the group are always in unspoken dialogue with one another. But for me, at least, the messy intimacy of this shared meal always turns such worries to background noise. This is part of what I loved at university and still love now about a feast of takeaway pizzas. However much people try to complicate or elevate it, it remains defiantly uncivilis-able. The streets of Naples sticking to our fingers, binding us all together, letting us know we belong to each other, for a while at least.

Meal 2: Roast Beef, Carrot and Swede, Roast Potato, and Yorkshire Puddings

"Dinner's ready!" someone would scream up the stairs, and slowly we would assemble to eat it. It was always just the four of us—my brother, my mum, my dad, and me. These are the first shared meals I remember. Sausage and mashed potatoes, steak and kidney casserole, spaghetti Bolognese, corned beef hash, and sometimes on Sunday a proper roast dinner with all the trimmings. If every meal is a performance, then this might be the most banal performance of all. An everyday micro-drama of serving and eating and arguing repeated almost every single day. Through this everyday ritual we construct our idea of what a family is or what it should be, and we restate the relationships that turn a particular group of people in a particular house into one.

To my brother and me, though, dinner was just dinner. Our concern was with what the meal was and how much we were allowed to eat. Our family dinners seemed to us as solid and dependable as the table we ate them off. I never considered the effort that went into making them. I spent no time thinking about who did the cooking, who served the food, who got to eat

first. The fraught politics of domestic life were, perhaps predictably, entirely missed by my brother and me as we played in our
rooms or watched TV. So much of the labour of family meals
remained invisible, as did any debate as to whose responsibility
that labour was.

I never wondered whether my parents ever struggled. Never
worried they wouldn't have enough food to feed all of us. Never
considered if they ever came home from work too exhausted to
cook, wanting just to sprawl out on the sofa and have their dinner brought to them. My brother and I never noticed the quick-
fixes, the short cuts, the easy meals, the unlikely combinations
of ingredients salvaged from some last-minute rummage in the
back of the cupboard. My partner, Beckie, remembers how her
mum used to make her and her brother something she called
"picnic tea," where she'd lay out a blanket on the living room floor
and cover it with small morsels—some crisps, boiled eggs, a slice
of ham, a bit of cheese—so that they could sit down together and
pretend they were having a picnic. It was only years later that
Beckie realised this was just her mum's way of making a meal
out of the almost-nothing she had left in the house. A way of
dressing up scraps and leftovers as a substantial meal. To Beckie
these imaginary picnics were a genuine treat—something her
mum surely only reserved for days when her and her brother
had been especially good.

Generally, children don't have a lot of say in what food is
served to them, how much they are served, or who does the
serving, which leaves really only one way to exert any degree of

agency or individuality, and that is by choosing which parts of the meal you'll eat willingly and which parts you won't.

As a child, being picky about what you eat is about more than deciding which foods you like and which you don't. It is a means of expression, a form of insurrection, perhaps even a kind of guerrilla warfare—a way of achieving some bodily autonomy within a space where you have virtually none. To be picky with food is part of the process of becoming an individual, with likes and dislikes that exist outside of the identity your parents have created for you. I love watching my friends' children being fussy with their food—picking the peas out of a bowl of pasta, demanding olives or capers or juicy green apple, staring at a blob of ketchup on their chips and crying, demanding a fork and then throwing the fork away. Their small acts of pointless rebellion fill me with a profound joy. I see you, unruly child! Busy with the business of self-invention! Claiming your tiny portion of freedom in the only way you know how! *Hasta la victoria siempre!*

Adults attempting to deal with this domestic rebellion seem to have developed a variety of tactics. There is the hard-line approach taken by cruel grandmas and terrifying aunts the world over—refusal to compromise, demanding full compliance or else there will consequences. There is the cajoling, the gamification; spoons that become choo-choo trains shuttling towards intransigent mouths. There is bribery, the promise of iPads and desserts if only you'll eat your peas. My mum tells me on the phone that her approach with my brother and me was acceptance of any pickiness as long as we had actually tried the thing we were refusing to eat. And so my dislike of peas and mushrooms and, worst of all, mashed carrot and swede was accepted by her only once I had performed my dislike of them; sticking a piece grudgingly in my mouth and then twisting my face up in disgust.

And then there are the more creative solutions. On the food podcast *Proof,* the writer Ahmed Ali Akbar tells a wonderful story about his mother and sisters' attempts to get him to eat his mother's Pakistani cooking by pretending it came from a new takeaway place in town called Pakistani Chicken Hut. Each time they would parcel the food up in takeaway boxes, place it in a paper bag, and one of his sisters would deliver it to the front door. Suddenly the food Ahmed would normally refuse to eat became a delicious treat, something he suggests was at least partly about his own attempts to navigate a fraught sense of identity as the first member of his immediate family not to be born in Pakistan. Somehow the idea of a takeaway shop (part KFC, part Pizza Hut, part Pakistani cooking) helped resolve his sense of cultural dissonance, creating a dinner that was just as American and Pakistani as he was. Like the stories we act out around Santa Claus or the Tooth Fairy, it isn't clear even to Ahmed how much this was something he believed and how much it was a game they were all playing together—a performance of belonging and becoming, a family and its food in the process of reimagining themselves..

This story also speaks to the anxiety that often sits just under the surface of the family meal—all those fears about the way our family compares to the other families. Insecurities about class, culture, and identity that often manifest in worries about whether we're eating properly, sitting in the right places, saying the right things to each other, behaving in the way a family is supposed to be behave.

Haunting all these fears is the spectre of the proper family meal, one eaten together around the dinner table, everyone talking politely, passing each other the salt, like a living Norman Rockwell painting. A paradigm of middle-class prosperity and respectability. In one of the earliest episodes of *The Simpsons*, Homer watches in horror as Marge, Lisa and Bart eat their dinner in front of the TV, shovelling food into their mouths with their eyes glued on the screen in front of them. Later they all sneak up to the window of a neighbour's house and watch them eating their dinner politely around a table—a picture of respectability and decorum, everything the Simpsons supposedly are not. The implication is clear: the way the Simpsons eat their dinner is indicative of their failure as a family. And presumedly when President George H. W. Bush famously demanded that American families behave "a lot more like the Waltons and a lot less like the Simpsons," implicit in that demand was an expectation that a proper family eats its dinner around the table rather than on their laps in front of the television.

But we don't need George H. W. Bush to tell us that this is how a good family should eat. A Google image search for "family dinner" brings up page after page of wooden tables laden with food. Mothers and fathers and children gazing lovingly at each other. Grandparents laughing. Everyone chinking glasses. Helping themselves to another portion of spaghetti or an extra spoonful of salad. *This is what a proper family meal looks like.* Side salads and freshly cut bread. Sunshine spilling in through the bay window. *This is how a proper family behaves.*

In my house we were a TV dinner kind of a family, shovelling food into our mouths with our eyes fixed on *Patriot Games* or *Air Force One* or whichever '90s thriller we had rented from Blockbuster that night. Maintaining a running commentary on the action between mouthfuls. Eating the peas first to get them out of the way. Picking the last potato off my mum's plate, which she claimed she couldn't finish but had probably saved especially for me.

I regret not a single second of any of those meals. We might not have been saying grace or discussing the issues of the day, but we had our own banal rituals. Dinner was an encounter in which we learnt to share food and share time with each other, however fleeting. One of the ways we learnt together what kind of family we were, or could be.

Meal 3: Goat's Cheese Roasted in Post-coital Sadness

Baroness Marie-Hélène de Rothschild was the kind of outlandish high-society figure who gets a thirteen-paragraph *New York Times* obituary simply for throwing parties. Over the course of four decades she made entertaining into an art form. Between 1959 and 1975 she held her most extravagant events at the family's vast château in Ferrières, with its eighty guest suites and space for a hundred servants, and her recognised masterpiece from this period was the Surrealist Ball.

On a December night in 1972 she invited 150 guests to make the short trip from Paris to join her and her husband for dinner, with a dress code of black tie and surrealist heads. The wealthy and the beautiful piled up like characters in a Bob Dylan song— over there, Audrey Hepburn smiling from inside a delicate wicker birdcage, talking with Alexis von Rosenberg, Baron de Redé, who was himself wearing an oversized top hat decorated with the face of the Mona Lisa. In a corner of the room, leaning back in his chair and stroking the end of a waxed moustache, was Salvador Dalí, dressed as Salvador Dalí. And at the centre of it all was Baroness Rothschild herself, posing for photographs wearing a pale blue silk ball gown and a full stag's head adorned with gold antlers and tears made from real diamonds.

The Surrealist Ball was a work of art. A piece of theatre. And Baroness Marie-Hélène seems to have understood very well the idea that a theatrical event begins the first moment you hear about it and doesn't end until the last time someone thinks about it.

This dinner began not with the serving of food, but with the arrival of one of the baroness's invitations—the soft thud of expensive card landing on thick carpet, opened to reveal fluffy white Magritte clouds floating in a beautiful cerulean sky. We might think of everything from that moment onwards as part of this encounter—all that worrying over just the right mask to wear, the puzzling over who else might be present, the journey through the Parisian night, the château lit up against the dark winter sky by a battery of floodlights, the footmen dressed as cats pretending to sleep on the central staircase, the furry plates, the fishes for forks, the menus listing "extra lucid" soup and goat's cheese roasted in "post-coital sadness." The champagne-feathered memories of the night, the anecdotes retold in the finest restaurants, reports in society magazines, the same details breathlessly recounted again and again on art and design forums or in online articles about the most famous dinner parties in history. All of this is as much a part of the event as the simple act of eating together.

This was the theatre of Marie-Hélène de Rothschild—"Society's Star Choreographer," as the headline in that *New York Times* obituary described her. These were the means she used to establish a shared social reality for herself and her guests—a way of being together in time. According to Alice Julier, a dinner party is a kind of performance through which "participants establish who they are in relation to each other and to the larger world." All those clever masks and headpieces, the suits and dresses, the expense, the exclusivity, the too-muchness of it all. What were these people—the movie stars and the millionaires and minor members of various European royal families—trying to tell each other about themselves? That they were interesting and sophisticated, for one thing, up on all the latest trends. One woman's costume involved an apple dangling in front of her face in homage to René Magritte's *The Son of Man*, a painting that was just eight years old at the time.

But there is something else going on beneath all of this, a note of fear and defiance, perhaps. Only four years earlier, Paris was on fire. Students rioting in the streets. Barricades. A general strike. Government officials burning documents and considering the quickest way to the border. A country on the precipice of revolution. "*Soyez réalistes, demandez l'impossible*," read the slogan written on the city's walls. The tenets of Dadaism and surrealism were buried deep in the bone marrow of May '68—their exhortation to destabilise reality, to make the impossible the only logical possibility. By rendering surrealism as pure surface—as costume and place setting and decoration, a celebrity meet-and-greet with Salvador Dalí himself—the guests at the Surrealist Ball attempted to draw the sting out of it. To return to a world in which strangeness and absurdity are just fancies adorning a reality that is comfortingly immutable.

Imagine them all there, drinking the finest champagne, silver spoons dipping into their goat's cheese in its post-coital sadness, tiny figures in a Fabergé snow globe. Their world is long gone now. Almost everyone who attended is now dead; Marie-Hélène herself died over a quarter of a century ago, in 1996. Only a few years after this party, the Rothschilds gave the Château de Ferrières to the university of Paris. It's now a cookery school.

Part of the allure of telling stories about such events is how wondrously distant they seem. How unlike our own lives the theatre of these elaborate events can appear. Extraordinary encounters in grand country houses, everyone dressed up like characters from a play. Or a film, perhaps. It is rumoured that the sinister masked ball in Stanley Kubrick's *Eyes Wide Shut* was inspired by the Surrealist Ball, filmed as it was in the Buckinghamshire country house upon which the Château de Ferrières was modelled. The rich and the beautiful of another age performing a version of the world they hope will last forever. A silken ritual of belonging for the 0.1 per cent.

And yet beneath the cartoon opulence, is there really all that much difference? Almost any dinner party is an attempt to build a social reality and then live inside it, like a play fort built on the lawn. And dinner parties remain a crucial form of social encounter for those with the means to host and attend them. These days the fashion is less towards theatrical excess and more towards displays of authenticity and modesty. More entertaining takes place in kitchens than it did forty years ago, and those kitchens are accordingly designed to be much larger than they once would have been, as this enables the hosts to prepare food in front of their guests. This is itself a kind of performance, as is the careful nonchalance of a casual WhatsApp invite, the pas de deux between host and guest over what they should bring with them ("just a bottle of wine and your good selves"), the choice of music, the post-event Instagram selfie.

We may not have the money or the audacity of Baroness Marie-Hélène de Rothschild, but whenever we have some people round for dinner, we are in our own small ways attempting to make all the uncertainties of the world and our place within it feel solid and unchanging, for at least the length of an evening.

Meal 4: Strawberries Dipped in Melted Chocolate

I still remember the time a man bit me on the finger as I was trying to feed him a strawberry. For his sake and mine, I have always assumed it was an accident, though I cannot know for sure. The strawberry was a dessert course and the wine had been flowing freely, so all the guests were pretty drunk by this point. I was also underneath the dining table at the time, my hand reaching up through a specially cut hole, appearing in the room like a disembodied limb, some ghoulish new piece of living cutlery, plucking food from the plate and placing it straight into the diner's mouth.

There were about ten of us under there, crouched in the darkness, each assigned a guest to feed. I cannot remember how much practice we had had, but I am sure it wasn't enough. It is harder than you'd think to collect an unseen strawberry from a plate, dip it into a bowl of melted chocolate, and then present it, ready for consumption. The bite happened after about the third strawberry. A sharp and unexpected pain as this stranger's teeth embedded themselves in the side of my index finger, not deep enough to draw blood but enough to leave a bruise. When finally we emerged from under the table to serve the rest of the meal, I couldn't look him in the eye.

The strawberries dipped in melted chocolate were about the fifth course in a tasting menu designed by the artist Charlotte Jarvis for a private dinner in the front room of a gallery on Whitecross Street in central London. This was 2009, and Charlotte was my flatmate at the time. We lived together with seven other people on the top floor of an empty office building in Walthamstow which she would occasionally turn into a secret restaurant serving high-concept meals—and side portions of experimental performance—to up to thirty paying guests at a time. I remember in particular a Christmas-themed dinner where I had to dress as an elf and help a gin-soaked Santa to stumble around the room, delivering presents. We were living through what was, with hindsight, the golden age of the secret restaurant in London—an era of pop-up dinners in abandoned churches and empty warehouses, speakeasy-style dining rooms hidden behind fake bookshelves. I remember a whole restaurant, replete with its own tiny wooden mezzanine level, squeezed inside an ordinary flat on a cobbled back street in Hackney; an ornate gastronomic universe concealed behind an unremarkable pale blue door.

The first restaurants appeared in the bustling cities of Song dynasty China around eight hundred years ago, and from the beginning they were recognised by their clientele as a new kind of metropolitan entertainment. Food no longer as merely sustenance or celebration, but a form of recreation. According to writers Katie Rawson and Elliott Shore, some of the earliest of these Chinese restaurants were located in entertainment districts and provided their customers with various forms of performance to accompany their meal, ranging from singing waiters to full theatrical productions—a kind of nascent dinner theatre.

In Europe it took until the gas and electric light of the nineteenth century to truly create a restaurant culture, when the night was transformed from a place of darkness to a bourgeois playground—a place to see and be seen. A restaurant, then, should be understood as, by definition, a place where the act of eating together has been commodified, transformed into a form of leisure for those who can afford it. Where there are people at leisure there are also, usually, people at work enabling that leisure. In restaurants these people share the same intimate space, moving around and past one another, pleasure and labour separated by little more than the width of a menu or a napkin, and sometimes not even that.

The relationship between those who are working and those who aren't is a source of discomfort that we try and alleviate through an array of polite social conventions and over-familiar jokes—unwritten rules around tipping that vary from place to place, jokes about rude customers and the hidden secrets their food contains, exhortations to thank your waiter, all those strained attempts to make eye contact in hope of receiving some service. Attempts to mitigate the complicated question of what it means to serve and be served. To put it out of our mind to better enjoy our meal. After all, would a steak be enjoyed as much if it came accompanied by a video documenting the working conditions of everyone involved in cooking it? Would the cocktails go down as smoothly if served on a copy of the mixologists' payslip?

Perhaps understandably, most restaurateurs design their restaurants to satisfy a simple idea of pleasure and entertainment. But for Charlotte, I think, pleasure is as much a function of discomfort and transgression as it is relaxation and satisfaction.

146

Ever since I have known her she has had a desire to peer into the darkness and see what she can find there, and her experiments in dining have always reflected this. There was, for example, the time she served a black pudding made from her own blood, or the time when she staged a meal in the window of a Cypriot art gallery, with passers-by invited to gaze in at diners as they ate their meals.

At the dinner on Whitecross Street, one course required audience members to serve each other from teaspoons with metre-long handles, whilst a pasta course was accompanied by a close-up film of a mouth loudly chewing and a sushi course was served on the naked body of a male performer who, once the course was completed, stood up, dressed, and joined the diners at the table, transgressing that separation between those who serve and those who are served, shifting uncomfortably between person and object in front of the other diners' eyes.

And then there were the chocolate strawberries. There was laughter and surprise when all of our hands burst in unison through the white paper tablecloth. It was funny, and kind of charming—surreal, even—all these hands moving across the dinner table like creatures in some cartoon ballet. And then the feeding began. Delicate fingers offered up to open mouths. An aphrodisiacal treat presented in the most intimate and sensuous of fashions. And yet, at the same time, it was all so remote, so dislocated. All of us hidden away in the folds of the table. Dismembered arms going wordlessly through the motions. All the tenderness and the tension of serving and being served, rendered in these absurd primary colours. I can still feel where the bite was on my finger, that little grey bruise it left behind, just by the second knuckle.

Meal 5: A Single Rolo

A Rolo is a small, round, chocolate caramel. A little knuckle-sized treat sold in packets of eleven, wrapped in gold foil and a familiar brown label with the word *ROLO* emblazoned along the side in bright red letters. As far as mass-market confectionery goes, Rolos are, I think, basically fine, no better or worse than Maltesers or Hershey's Kisses or M&M's. But the thing everyone knows about Rolos—or at least everyone who grew up in the UK in the 1980s and 1990s knows—is that they are the simplest and most perfect expression of love widely available to the general public for under a pound. We know this because television told us it was so.

For over twenty years, from 1980 to 2003, Rolos were advertised with the question "Do you love anyone enough to give them your last Rolo?" It was featured in billboards and magazine ads and on television, first through a ten-year-long series of adverts featuring a cartoon couple who diligently saved their last Rolos for each other as a symbol of their forever love, and then through yet more adverts that subverted this formula: a boy refusing to give his last Rolo to an elephant, a couple on a train journey agonising over who gets to eat the last Rolo before one of them steals it away as they rush through a dark tunnel. Over time the notion that sharing your last Rolo is a profound romantic gesture burrowed its way into our collective subconscious. There are few simpler romantic encounters, which is perhaps why, for people of my generation, it stuck so hard. Even now no one I know could open a packet of Rolos without some commentary about the final destination of the last one. A little corner of our cultural memory colonised by Nestlé.

Sharing food is a basic behaviour, one that entangles us humans back up with our animal selves. We, like many species, share food with our young because otherwise they will die. We also, like many species, occasionally share food with other adults. Lots of birds—robins, blue jays, terns—practise what is known as courtship feeding, with one bird, usually a male, finding food and then bringing it back to share with their mate. Although, as the British Trust for Ornithology website makes clear, the term *courtship feeding* is generally something of a misnomer. These birds are not performing courtship. Instead, this behaviour is usually employed by male birds "as a means of increasing the incubation intensity of their mates to bring forward hatching," which increases the offspring's chances of survival.

Primates also often share food, and here doing so tends to be less directly grounded in biological expediency and is more akin to grooming and other sorts of behaviour that help establish ties between individual members of a larger group. In nonmonogamous species like chimpanzees and orangutans, sharing food often occurs in the short periods during which males and females are breeding, whilst in some monogamous species, like owl monkeys, food sharing takes place after breeding as well, whilst the pairs are raising their offspring. Here there is more of a symbolic or gestural quality to the action of sharing food. Food offered and accepted as a tool for bonding, perhaps even as a sign of affection. A shiver of something we might recognise as romance.

Evidence seems to suggest that early humans shared food for similar reasons—hunters demonstrating their skill as hunters, their ability to provide for their dependents. In some extant hunter-gatherer communities, hunters will choose a more difficult prey over an easier one and offer it up as evidence of their strength and skill. This is food intimately associated with courtship, and, concomitantly, with mating. Sharing a meal as a precursor to something even more carnal.

Food and sex. Sex and food. Sexy food. Foody encounters defined by acts of aphrodisiacal consumption. This collision of desires is one of the places out of which chocolate first emerged. The Aztec emperor Montezuma II would supposedly drink cup after foaming cup of cacao as a prelude to bouts of riotous love-making, and from the time that the Spanish first brought it to Europe, chocolate was revered amongst the upper classes as a sexual stimulant. Charles II spent more money each year on chocolate than he did on his mistress. Over time the association of chocolate with the sexual voraciousness of the European aristocracy was diluted and commodified so that, by the 1860s, Victorian chocolatiers were mass-producing chocolate boxes for the middle classes to share on Valentine's Day. Here, the sharing of food had been entirely domesticated—rendered largely a symbolic gesture, in keeping with an era, and a class, preoccupied with decorum and respectability.

An offering of chocolates is an encounter in which desire is shrouded in metaphor, and no food is quite as metaphorical as chocolate: all longing, opulence, and desire condensed into uniform squares of mass-produced confectionery. Hot blood pumping through heart-shaped boxes.

Which brings us back to the last Rolo. That most purely symbolic of all food-based gifts. The sharing of food elevated to the status of bad poetry. Not even a whole heart-shaped box. Just a single bite's worth, and in some cases not even that. In 2017 the UK's *Daily Mail* newspaper reported on a woman called Lynne Brooks from Stinchcombe, Gloucestershire, who had saved the last Rolo that her now-husband Richard had given to her on their first Valentine's Day date in 1984. For the last thirty years it had remained in a wooden box, now little more than a crater of flaky, blackened chocolate, taken out occasionally to show friends and family. "We both like Rolos," Lynne is quoted in the article as saying. "Even now he would still give me his last Rolo and I would always do the same for him."

I don't know if I have ever personally bought a packet of

Rolos, but I want you to know that were I to do so, I would always give away my last one. I would share it with whomever is nearby: lover or stranger, friend or foe. I would share it with you were we ever to meet. I promise you this. I have so much love to give and I will give it all, one chocolate caramel at a time.

Meal 6: Biryani, Samosa, Chickpea Masala, Kebab, and Dates

They began preparing the meal just before dusk, the June sun dipping beneath the houses and the cloudless sky turning a deeper shade of blue. St Thomas's Road in the Finsbury Park area of North London was closed to traffic and a lime green tablecloth laid along the centre of the road. Bunting was strung up between the houses on each side of the street. Bottles of water laid out, ready to quench a thirst that had been building all day. Volunteers from Muslim Aid bustled around in green T-shirts as people began to arrive. The street Iftar was scheduled to begin at 8 p.m. with speeches by local politicians and community leaders, before the free food was served just after the sun set at around nine o'clock. Biryani, samosa, chickpea masala, kebab, and dates. Everyone was welcome to attend. "An Iftar is the sunset meal which breaks the Ramadan fast each day," Muslim Aid advised those who might not be familiar with the custom. "It is tradition-ally eaten within a large family or group gathering."

Fasting is one of the five central pillars of Islam. The Rama-dan fast takes place each year for the duration of the ninth month of the Islamic calendar, when Muslims abstain from food or drink between sunrise and sunset, the fast ending each night with the Iftar. The Qur'an contains detailed descriptions of the practice, indicating that its roots extend back to nearly the earliest days of Islam. In Judaism and Christianity, too, fasting of different kinds is an important ritual observance. In Cherokee spiritualism, fasting is one of the ways of invoking the aid of the river, Yun'wi Gunahi'ta—"the long man." As a religious observance, fasting is about the power of restraint—as a test of faith, an expression of piety or sometimes of penitence. More than anything it is an act of overcoming. And the breaking of a fast is a celebration of this overcoming, a recognition both of our strength and our fragility. It is an expression of our essential humanness, our ability to persevere. And persevering is easier when it is done together.

In 2017 Oxford University psychology professor Robin Dunbar examined people's eating habits as they related to a range of social and individual benefits. Using information from two thousand respondents to a nationwide survey who monitored their eating habits for a seven-day period, he looked at the impact of eating socially across five key social indices—"engaged with the local community, level of trust in local community, worthwhileness of life, happiness on day before and satisfaction with life." What he found was that in all cases, "those who ate socially at least sometimes gave significantly higher ratings than those who always ate alone." He concluded that not only are "people who eat socially more likely to feel better about themselves and to have a wider social network capable of providing social and emotional support," but that "eating together may have health and survival benefits both directly and, through bigger and better social networks, indirectly." Persevering really is easier when it is done together.

This no doubt explains the long history of social eating across the world, as far back as the some of the earliest organised societies. There is, for example, evidence that some workers in early Sumerian cities were paid in food served from a big communal pot. In many cultures the end of harvest is still accompanied by a festival that involves celebratory communal feasting—in England in the sixteenth century, carts full of food would roll through the streets of the town led by an appointed "harvest lord." Even today there are thriving street food cultures across the world; on any walk through the woozy heat of a Bangkok evening, you will pass dozens of street food vendors selling sizzling morsels of chicken, pork, and squid on little wooden sticks, all for little more than a few pence each.

And yet, increasingly, there are also crushing inequalities in the way we eat, and in many places eating socially has consequently become a kind of privilege. Eating out can be expensive, even something like a Domino's pizza or a McDonald's hamburger remains out of reach of many families. At the same time, an invitation to someone's house for dinner usually comes with an expectation that at some point you will return the favour. People who can't do so, for reasons of money or space or the precarious nature of their circumstances, are less likely to accept an offer of dinner. As I write this, the UK is going through an energy crisis in which it is being reported that some food banks are requesting donations of food which does not require cooking, because people can't afford the gas or electricity to cook it. If people cannot even cook for themselves, what hope do they have of being able to cook for others?

If the ability to eat socially is out of the reach of many people, then so too are the benefits that accrue from doing so. Eating together, which should be a source of solidarity and collective strength, becomes another way in which societal divisions are consolidated and privilege reinforced. All of which doesn't even begin to cover the range of other factors—the complexities of gender and race, the fact of living within a fundamentally fatphobic society—that affect people's ability to eat with or in front of others.

We are living through a time of accumulating crises, and things are likely to only get more difficult and more divisive. Eating together should be a source of respite. A way of persevering together, rather than another source of division.

In her book *A Paradise Built in Hell*, Rebecca Solnit tells the story of the Mizpah Café, a temporary soup kitchen stitched together from blankets, carpets, and bedsheets in Golden Gate Park in the immediate aftermath of the San Francisco earthquake of 1906. Whilst the fire that consumed the city still raged on in the background, the café's proprietor, Anna Amelia Holshouser, began serving the survivors clustering in the park, eventually feeding up to three hundred people a day. Above the entrance to the Mizpah Café a hand-painted sign read, "One Touch of Nature Makes the Whole World Kin." In the darkness of those nights, they would gather to eat together, people stripped of their station and their status, their old world temporarily suspended, a new one being forged amongst the scattered tents and other makeshift refuges. It was, according to Solnit, a time of sadness but also of great joy. "Imagine a society," she writes, "where money plays little or no role, where people rescue each other and then care for each other, where food is given away, where life is mostly out of doors in public, where the old divides between people seem to have fallen away, and the fate that faces them, no matter how grim, is far less so for being shared."

The Finsbury Park street Iftar of 2018 was also, in a very different way, a gathering of people in the aftermath of a disaster. A place where people came to care for each other and food was given away to anyone who wanted it. The event took place one year on from a terrorist atrocity on the same street, when a white van was deliberately driven into a group of Muslim worshippers who had recently left the Finsbury Park Mosque and were attempting to administer first aid to a man, Makram Ali, who had collapsed at a bus stop. Makram Ali later died as a result of the attack. This terrible incident occurred within a febrile atmosphere in London in particular and the UK in general. The Islamophobia of the right-wing press, combined with an anti-immigrant sentiment unleashed by the Brexit referendum, had fostered an environment of hostility and mistrust that worked its way into the gaps in already fractured communities.

The Iftar was billed by organisers as an attempt to celebrate the way the Finsbury Park community came together in the aftermath of this Islamophobic attack, but more generally it spoke to a desire to try and mend that which had seemed broken. The organisers' invitation cleverly elided British values and the teachings of Islam, a subtle riposte to those people who like to promote the idea of a divisive "clash of civilisations." "We are really looking forward to sharing with neighbours who are of faith or no faith," they said, "bringing mosques, synagogues, churches together and local leadership. Islam is about sharing everything with your neighbours and Britain shows its true colours when everyone comes together." A British street party and a traditional Ramadan Iftar at one and the same time. A meal of pluralities. A beginning. A welcome.

Even those organisers must have been surprised, however, by quite how many people chose to turn up. Over two thousand in total, sitting together in the road, talking, eating, mourning, persevering. Enjoying something both new and old. Eating their dates and taking in the warm summer evening under that darkening cloudless sky.

CHAPTER 6

ECSTATIC ESCAPE

For now the nightclub is empty and the people who will fill it are scattered all over town. Some of them are in bedrooms trying on outfits, some of them smoking on balconies, others are pre-drinking in the corner of the bar. There are people dancing around their living rooms with the music turned up too loud, the strobe lights already flickering inside of them. And there are others who are watching TV or talking to their mum or having a bath. There are people rushing to finish their shift and others on the train into town. There are people buying drugs and others selling drugs. There are people sightseeing and there are people shopping, their hair already in rollers in anticipation of the night ahead.

These people are all already connected, though they don't know it yet. Haze and blue light and a phantom baseline already swirl around them, pulling them towards one another. They are caught in a knot that will slowly tighten over the next three hours until they are a single body, a many-headed monster, its thousand limbs all raised in the air. Twelve hours from now they will say they love each other, and they will really mean it. They will walk out into the dawn, arm in arm, lighting each other's cigarettes with shaky hands. The dance floor will be slick with sweat and spilt drinks, cans and cigarette butts, lost coins and tiny resealable bags.

But right now the dance floor holds none of these things. The lights are off. No one is around save for the bar staff doing their stock check and the cleaners slowly mopping their way across the room.

Movement I: To the Edgelands

We are off, heading towards the edges, to the outer limits of the city, or somewhere that feels to me like the outer limits of the city. To some hinterland of abandonment and decay where the street lights don't always work and the weeds are allowed to grow wild. Where the graffiti was painted more recently than the road markings. Zones of inattention, where the expensive cloth of the modern metropolis sags and tatters until something more feral can be seen through it. Places of uncertainty and possibility that we travel to in search of rooms of flickering light and surging noise; rooms in which we can lose ourselves amidst a warm throng of dancing bodies.

It is 2008 and we are squeezed into the back of a minicab on our way to Hackney Wick, a clutter of former industrial units and oily garages in the nowhere space between the A12 and the building site that will one day become London's gleaming new Olympic park. Apple have just launched the iPhone and we are living in the city's last great era of unnavigability, before its every granular detail will fold neatly into any pocket. We are watching through half-misted windows as the streets grow quieter and less familiar, interrogating the factories and warehouses for signs of life, wondering where it is we are going, winding down the windows to see if we can hear the sound of music playing.

Or it is 2012 and we are walking hand in hand through the streets of Berlin, along corridors of old concrete apartment blocks, breathing in the cold air. It is nearly midnight and we are heading west to east, through what was once the hard edge of the city, across a bridge over the Spree, where the wall once stood. We are just tourists here, trying not to look like tourists, walking with the nonchalance of people who know the city better than we actually do. Catherine wheels are spinning in the pit of my stomach but I'm trying my best not to show it.

Or I am walking alone through my hometown of Cambridge, past the city's polite, public face, its cobbles and its colleges. In my smartest red shirt and trainers, I am walking past the train station, the road rising up to traverse the railway lines. I can see in the distance a squat, square building with a queue of people snaking out of it. It is 2001, I am sixteen years old, and I am attempting to go out dancing for the first time. I've walked for nearly an hour to get here, and it could still be all for nothing.

Cities have always been at their wildest at the edges, in those

overlooked places of questionable legality and limited adminis-
trative oversight. In their neglect is buried a degree of freedom
not shared by the more cared-for and policed parts of a city. As
far back as the early 1600s Southwark, on the south bank of the
Thames, was London's disreputable playground, a marshy space
at the river's edge unbound by the regulations of the official city.
Ordinary people crossed the river in their thousands to enjoy
bear-baiting and dogfights, to drink, to gamble, and to squeeze
in their thousands into open-air theatres to watch the bawdy
and violent plays outlawed within the city's official limits. The
encounters people had in this outlaw space were infused with
both a danger and a sense of possibility that was not available to
them in the politer, more restricted zones within the city.

Around a hundred and fifty years later, on the other side of
the Atlantic, a very different kind of freedom was forged in an
empty, grass-covered field on the margins of New Orleans that
became known as Congo Square. Here, enslaved people gathered in the limited space and time available to them, initially to
sell crops they had cultivated, later to dance together. By the time
of the Louisiana Purchase at the beginning of the nineteenth
century, the square would be filled each weekend by hundreds
of dancers—enslaved people and free people of colour—and
the intermingling rhythms of various scattered groups of musi-
cians playing drums, gourds, banzas, violins, marimbas, trian-
gles, and other more improvised instruments made from cow
horns and horse teeth. Here on this bare patch of land, ances-
tral dances passed down through generations burst out into the

open. This space at the margins, clawed back temporarily from their oppressors, became a source of solidarity and belonging. Dancing together at the outer limits, these marginalised people were able to forge the beginnings of a completely new African American musical tradition. A new vision, even, of what America might be. The rattle and shake could be felt from streets away.

As cities have changed, so have their edgelands, becoming less tied to the geographical outskirts. In the second half of the twentieth century, Western cities' most obvious edge spaces often became their former industrial zones, emptied out by changing methods of production and transformed into an interior wilderness of cavernous, unloved buildings in search of a function. The low rent, superhuman scale, and relative isolation of these places made them ideal spaces for people to gather to dance.

In Chicago in the late '70s and early '80s, house music was born, taking its name from a club known as the Warehouse, a three-storey former factory on the edge of downtown which, twice a month, became an after-hours juice bar where hundreds of largely gay Black and Latino patrons would dance right through from midnight Saturday to midday Sunday. Modern club culture in the UK, meanwhile, was kick-started in Manchester in 1981 when Factory Records transformed an old red-brick yacht builders' warehouse into the Hacienda, an audaciously eccentric nightclub and gig venue that became a mecca for young people wanting to dance to these new sounds coming from America.

Venues like the Warehouse and the Hacienda created a

blueprint for a kind of experience. A seemingly indelible association between clubbing and the woozy hedonism and anti-
authoritarianism nurtured in these industrial edgelands, out of
sight and out of mind of the rest of the city. As an awkward,
undersized teenager in Cambridge in the late '90s I was very far
from either of these legendary venues, and yet going out dancing
still felt to me like something illicit, rebellious, and wondrously
strange. With a poorly doctored photocopy of my passport thrust
in my back pocket and the sickly-sweet taste of cheap alcopop in
my throat, I would set out towards a nightclub called the Junction, an intimidating concrete bunker at one corner of a vast
car park, queueing up nervously with all the other questionably
dressed would-be ravers, listening to the machine thump of a
music that was unlike anything in my parents' CD collection.
In reality the Junction might have been a council-funded community arts space barely a mile from the city centre, but to me
it was another universe.

I felt the same thrill a decade later when friends who knew
London better than me would take me to warehouse parties
in Hackney Wick, another imagined edgeland that felt much
farther from normality than it really was, or when my partner
first took me clubbing in Berlin. No matter the actual location
we were heading to, these all felt like journeys to the edge of
somewhere, or something. Journeys that we undertook as much
in hope as expectation, dreaming of flickering lights and surging
noise. Hoping to lose ourselves amidst all those dancing bodies.

Feel it now, if you can—the anticipation of all those bodies and all that noise, the tickly lightness of not knowing what the evening will entail.

Movement II: Crossing the Threshold

We wrap our coats around ourselves as light rain begins to fall. We are close enough now to hear the music, the twinkling treble dancing on the breeze and the bass line thud coming up through the gravel beneath our feet. Around us, other people are arriving too, drawn out of the night like moths, stepping from the backs of taxis, hands thrust deep in their pockets, heads already nodding to the music. Everyone seems as quietly, nervously excited as we are. We all walk the same way, together and not together, lost for now in our own private worlds, walking purposefully towards that parliament of lights just about visible in the distance.

It's 1 a.m. and the queue for entry into Berghain stretches back across bare concrete and grassy shrubland. There are maybe forty or fifty people in front of us, shuffling slowly, affecting a kind of studied indifference about their likelihood of getting past the world's most notoriously capricious door staff. Perhaps some of them genuinely are indifferent, veterans of the Berlin techno scene who, if turned away, will simply shrug and move on. It's hard to say what's real and what's performance. My own nonchalance, though, is certainly all for show. Inside, I am nothing but small birds trying desperately to get out.

Berghain is Berlin's most legendary techno club. A brutalist former power station where hundreds of people come to dance together every night to dark, alien beats thundering from an industrial-scale sound system. It takes its name from the two districts it straddles—Kreuzberg in the West and Friedrichshain in the East, foregrounding its seductive estrangement from the traditions and conventions of either half of the city surrounding it. I am with Beckie, who used to live in Berlin and has prepared me for the very real possibility that we won't get in this evening. Behind us we can hear the easy chatter of a group of young American students, but as per Beckie's instruction, we remain coolly impassive, drinking white wine straight from our tiny individual bottles, enjoying the sharpness as it swirls across our tongues.

A pilgrim is someone who sets out from the familiarity of home on a journey to a place that exists outside of the comfort and routine of their ordinary life in pursuit of an experience that will enrich them in some way, enabling them to understand the everyday world differently, before returning home to that ordinary life again. The pilgrimage is as old as antiquity, reoccurring in different guises across myriad societies. It is a ghost we carry inside ourselves, a profound longing that nearly all of us appear to share.

Whilst pilgrimage has historically been thought of as a religious rite, there are other secular journeys that take the same shape, from the visits fans make to the homes or gravesides of their favourite pop stars to the many Americans who travel each year to the Vietnam memorial in Washington. The anthropologist Victor Turner has suggested that a pilgrimage may be any journey that takes us out of the confines of ordinary society and our everyday lives, enabling us to experience a collective joy in the temporary community we form as pilgrims.

Let us for a moment, then, think of ourselves as pilgrims, all of us here in this queue in the cold of a Berlin November, or all the would-be dancers in any door queue anywhere in the world. They are all pilgrims. A crowd of pilgrims, a flock of them, shuffling meekly forward, swallowing their fear, their inebriated excitement, their nervous energy, hiding their drugs in their shoes and hiding their too-young faces behind layers of borrowed ennui. All of them caught together in this slightly tedious holding pattern between the ordinary society and the collective joy that they hope awaits them inside.

To think of this queue as part of a pilgrimage is to recognise what it does to us. It is to recognise it, perhaps, as a kind of performance, a dance before the dance, a way of establishing a sense of community and belonging that will be crucial to the togetherness we want to feel when we finally get inside. To think of the journey in this way is to understand one of the reasons why these slightly intimidating nightclubs make such perfect places to dance—they are places that require just enough effort to get into that it makes the experience feel sacred.

Getting into Berghain is so legendarily difficult that there are websites dedicated to teaching people how to do it. You can find out what time to arrive (very early or very late), who to come with (almost nobody), what clothes to wear (black casual), how much German to speak (some), and even how excited to seem whilst you are queueing (excited, but not, you know, *too* excited). But even if you do everything right, it may not be enough. As we near the front of the queue I can see some people being nodded in by the impassive bouncer, and others being politely but firmly told that they won't be coming in tonight.

As I stand there trying to look cool, I remember all my other failed attempts to gain entry to much less spectacular clubs than this one. The sophisticated dramaturgy my underage friends and I would employ to try and convince the door staff to let us in— pairing off girls and boys to give the impression we were all mature couples rather than an unruly gang of teenagers, oldest walking with youngest, anyone with a beard up front, wearing our most sophisticated coats, never looking the bouncer in the eye. We are now only a few people from the entrance. The Americans are still chattering away behind us—unwisely, I quietly think to myself. In front, the intimidating façade of the vast former industrial building looms like the gate of St Peter. In the narrow second-floor windows the silhouettes of dancing figures twinkle through the translucent glass that glows purple, then green, then blue.

The ordeal of Berghain's door policy is the most theatrical example of the way the journey to a club it transformed into a rite of passage; a ritual of shared belonging that helps create a temporary utopia beyond the threshold. But before you can even arrive at the queue, simply learning about a venue, party, or club night usually requires a certain amount of inside information, a recommendation from a friend that you in turn share with another friend, and link by link a community is formed around this semi-sacred knowledge.

Clubs are not normally well advertised or well signposted—their opacity is part of their allure. The Warehouse in Chicago was not officially called the Warehouse. There was no sign above the door, and in the early '80s no website or Google maps to guide you there. People sought it out because they wanted to dance to the music played by resident DJ Frankie Knuckles, and when he moved elsewhere, they followed. Today, as musical tastes continues to splinter and diversify, specialist websites like Resident Advisor help direct clubbers to whatever sound they might be looking for, even in the most obscure corners of the city.

These visible and invisible trials undoubtedly forge a sense of belonging among the successful pilgrims, but one that comes at the expense of accessibility, and always with the spectre of exclusion.

There have been egregious examples of nightclubs that use their door policies as an expression of elite power. In a notorious 2015 incident at Dstrkt nightclub in Leicester Square, a group of Black women were prevented from entering the club because their skin was too dark, setting off a moment of reckoning during which numerous people of colour shared their experience of racist door policies at similar high-end London clubs. Such exclusions are an act of violence perpetrated on people at the margins and demonstrate how such clubs see themselves as part of a system of exclusionary privilege. As Stormzy put it in his song "First Things First": "Fuck Dstrkt and fuck all these night-clubs, and fuck giving money to people that don't like us."

On its website, Dstrkt makes it very clear that it sees itself as part of a system of wealth and prestige long associated with the centre of the city, promoting itself as being only for "the most discerning clientele," a place to brush shoulders with "the famous and the fabulous." At the city's middle, close to the historic centre of elite power, exclusion is used to reinforce that power by suppressing and excluding the marginalised and unwanted.

On the margins, the threat of exclusion can have a very different purpose. Both the Warehouse and Berghain grew out of their respective cities' gay scenes, where the opportunity for communality, spontaneity, and joy in dancing was hard won and in need of protecting, and both clubs' opacity and inaccessibility might be best understood as ways of safeguarding the communities that they had helped create. Sven Marquardt, the head of security at Berghain, has described their door policy as a way of making the club "a safe place for people who come purely to enjoy the music and celebrate—to preserve it as a place where people can forget about space and time for a little while and enjoy themselves." Here, a lack of access is a promise to those inside that they will be kept safe.

But as well as creating a space of security for a community of dancers, such policies also have the effect of helping shape and perpetuate that community. They become part of the pilgrimage people undertake to get there. The sacred rite they submit themselves to. It may not always be as obvious as Berghain, but in door queues everywhere people rehearse how to act, how to dress, how to wear their hair, how to hold a cigarette just so. Like shoaling fish, they remake themselves in relation to the collective, and by doing so inherit an embodied knowledge passed down through generations of dancers. They play the role of someone who belongs until they are successful enough at doing so that they actually belong.

In the dark of the Berlin night, the bouncer looks us up and down and unsmilingly gestures for us to head inside. We cross the threshold. My heart is an airbag exploding on impact. We open the doors and there they all are. Bodies moving in the darkness. The music roars.

Movement III: A Succession of Repetitive Beats

Dancing together might be the oldest way we have of not feeling afraid. A way of keeping at bay the unknowability of the world and all the dangers it may or may not contain.

At the height of the wet season in Gombe National Park in Tanzania, when raindrops waterfall from the sky, splatting across low-hanging leaves and the forest floor, chimpanzees have been observed to strut and sway along to the sound, striding across the ground in big, looping figure eights, matching their own furious energy to that of the weather. Primatologists who study chimpanzees believe that our own human dancing might have evolved from this kind of behaviour. Yuko Hattori from Kyoto University, for example, speculates that animals like chimps began making rhythmic patterns of sound as a coping mechanism when faced with loud and overwhelming stimuli in the world around them. Over time we learnt how to combine this rhythmic sound with movement, honing the way we moved and rhythms that we move to, slowly building the origins of something resembling the way we dance to music today.

There is something wonderful about the idea that music and dance may have originated as a way of coping with the often-overwhelming experience of simply being in the world. A means of reflecting and refashioning all the noise and the chaos, the riot of a thunderstorm, the fury of a stampede, the sudden shock of a rockfall or an avalanche. A way to bundle it all up in sound and dance it into oblivion. Dance until we aren't afraid any more.

We have been dancing for so long now. We have danced through ice ages and migrations. Through droughts and floods and famines. We danced through extinctions and wars of ever-greater scale and sophistication. Through revolutions, colonisations, enslavements. We danced through the Black Death and smallpox and cholera. We danced through the Industrial Revolution.

We danced into the Machine Age, when the way we lived was transformed forever by the power of capital. When, as philosopher Simone Weil observed, the oscillations and variations of our natural rhythms were supplanted by the clockwork repetition of industrial time. When we started to be woken up by the clock and not the dawn, when time itself was standardised and contained. When our bodies were repurposed as cogs within the infinite machine of capitalism. Writing about her time working on an assembly line in the 1930s, Weil described how our capacity to move in our own way, and especially our capacity to pause, was broken by the brutal mechanical cadence of the factory, which demanded that workers labour ever more quickly and productively, a "miserable precipitation that spoils them of any grace and dignity." Even now our lives continue to be governed by these unrelenting mechanical rhythms, the beep of the alarm clock every morning, the nine-to-five grind, the repetitious actions and movements that structure so many different kinds of working day, from supermarket checkouts to Amazon warehouses, the compulsion to move faster, work harder, achieve more, consume more.

Now in our vast modern cities it is rarely the sound of rainstorms or stampedes that overwhelms us, but rather the sound of so many other people, driving cars, talking on their phones, shouting, arguing, fighting, working, living right up against one another. More than anything, the thing people learn to be afraid of is each other, and especially of those people they identify as different to themselves, as "other." This fear is reinforced in particular in big, densely populated cities, where people from different backgrounds and communities live in intimate proximity to one another. Such places are characterised as especially dangerous; hotbeds of violent crime, hostility, and mutual suspicion. This was especially true in the late 1970s and 1980s, when in places like Chicago, Manchester, and Detroit the decline of industry and the hollowing-out of the inner cities helped foster a conception, fuelled by prejudice and neglect, of urban life as perpetually blighted by criminality and violence.

It is no coincidence that such cities were the first places where people, especially those "marked as other," including people of colour and queer people, came together to create a new music and a new way of dancing together that reflected and refashioned this new reality. That took our paranoic urban isolation and its relentless machine rhythms and made a new kind of machine music to enable them to cope with it.

The 1986 Chicago house song "Your Love" begins with a simple three-note arpeggio synth loop, tiny pricks of sound descending out of the darkness like rain falling on a still pond. A few seconds later a drum machine erupts; snare, kick drum, and a barely perceptible high hat combine to create a propulsive beat that you feel as a snap in your shoulders, along your spine, down the backs of your legs. This is followed almost immediately by a sparse bass synth loop that carves itself a hole in your chest and takes up residence there. This song isn't so much moving forward as orbiting, accumulating new textures, new rhythms, new feelings as it does so. Then, at about the one-minute mark, a single sustained string note unfurls like a fog bank, wrapping itself around the first three sounds, binding everything together. There are a number of versions of this song, each combining these four elements in a slightly different way, but every one I've heard begins with that initial three-note synth line, looping and looping, insistently, unchangingly; a rippling, repetitive pulse that cannot be denied.

Before it was a house track, "Your Love" was a poem and then a three-minute love song. The track was written and recorded by Jamie Principle, who was, at the age of twenty-five, already a veteran of Chicago's early house scene. The track ended up in the hands of Frankie Knuckles, the godfather of house music, who had by then moved from the Warehouse to his own club, the Power Plant, based in a former industrial unit near the much-maligned Cabrini-Green housing project. Frankie added the drum machine and those rippling synths, stretching the song out into an extended six-or-seven-minute odyssey that broke in waves over the dancers at the Power Plant, moving them first one way and then another, a swirling, eddying current of sound. Because the thing you may not notice about "Your Love" as it soaks through your skin is that the initial three-note synth line is in a completely different time signature to the rest of the song, meaning it is constantly changing location in relation to the other elements of the track, twisting itself around those repetitive machine beats like an act of seduction.

In this music, repetition becomes a texture rather than a condition; it bends and dips and unfurls, it pauses and recommences, it moves in wondrous ways, and the dancers move along with it. This new machine music transformed the deadening cadence of mechanical repetition into something vibrant, sensuous, and alive. In the ruined cathedrals of our industrial age, in buildings where once thousands of people had performed the same repetitive tasks hour after hour, day after day, in the production of profit for a tiny few, people now gathered to dance in glorious, defiant unproductivity.

Just as we have always done, we took all the noise of the world and made it something we could dance to together—a small act of overcoming. In Detroit, the originators of techno called this "reprogramming." "Isn't it obvious that music and dance are the keys to the universe?" asked the manifesto of the music collective Underground Resistance. "So-called primitive animals and tribal humans have known this for thousands of years!"

Still today, I think this is why people go. It is why they venture to these spaces that exist away from the comfort of their ordinary lives, whether it be a converted factory on the outskirts of town or a basement club two doors down from them. It is why I will queue in the Berlin rain for over an hour, knowing the whole time I might not even be allowed in. Because in these darkened rooms, as we move together, we are teaching ourselves how not to be afraid of one another.

On YouTube you can watch a clip of "Your Love" being played at an illegal rave at Raydon Airfield in Essex in 1989. It sounds garbled and distorted, like it's been played at the other end of a tunnel that's three decades long, but still those twinkling synths are unmistakable. In the incongruous brightness of an aircraft hangar in the middle of the day, people move in circles, their arms tracing weird patterns in the air. A woman in a black top, black hat, and sunglasses bobs in the centre of the frame, gold hoop earrings swinging as she glitches backwards and forwards like an old video game on pause. Even so far removed, you can feel the heat of the bodies spinning and jumping and sometimes just walking, moving past and through and around one another. At one point there is a pause. The beat temporarily drops out, and in the space where the music was, you can hear the sound of the room and all the people in the room, and when they hear that sound, everybody cheers.

Movement IV: Ecstasy

The other thing I could have said about all the people in that YouTube clip is that they look like they have probably taken quite a lot of drugs.

Ecstasy is a name that became attached in the 1980s to 3,4-methylenedioxymethamphetamine, or MDMA, a drug first synthesised by the German pharmaceutical company Merck in 1912 and then largely forgotten about until picked up in the late '60s and early '70s by a network of American scientists who recognised its mood-altering effects, christening it "Adam" in reference to the Edenic state it engendered.

From its earliest recreational use, ecstasy has been associated with empathy. Alexander Shulgin, the California scientist who rediscovered it in 1966, labelled it an "empathogen," whilst in their book *Altered States*, Matthew Collin and John Godfrey quote an American researcher telling them that "the man who first named it 'Ecstasy' told me that he chose the name because it would sell better than calling it 'Empathy.' 'Empathy' would be more appropriate, but how many people know what it means?"

MDMA appears to work by enhancing the positive and dampening the negative in our experience of our environment, in particular in our relationship to the people around us. A study in 2012 demonstrated that people on MDMA improved in their ability to recognise positive emotions in others, but became significantly worse at recognising negative or threat-related expressions, instead mistaking them for friendly ones. Another study in 2014 which involved participants playing a virtual game of catch similarly identified an impaired ability to recognise hostility and rejection in people who had taken the drug, which resulted in a feeling of positivity and "love" for those around them. If scientists had actively set out to create a designer drug to counter the paranoic effect of the contemporary urban experience, they couldn't have done much better than MDMA. Collin and Godfrey frame ecstasy as another facet of club culture's social reprogramming, a kind of ghost in Thatcher's machine "expressing desires for a collective experience that Thatcher rejected and consumerism could not provide."

In her book *Trick Mirror*, Jia Tolentino associates the feeling of taking MDMA with the kind of religious ecstasy she encountered in her early childhood growing up in a megachurch in Houston, another kind of vast, cavernous space where people come together to defy alienation and feel some greater sense of connection to one another. To be on ecstasy is to be 'like a child of Jesus,'" she writes. "You feel that your soul is dazzling, delicate, unlimited; you understand that you can give yourself away to everyone you love without ever feeling depleted."

Ecstasy, as it was originally understood by early mystical writers, referred to a state of rapture that "stupefied the body while the soul contemplated divine things." What Tolentino is describing is in some ways the opposite of this, an experience in which you feel more fully present in your body than ever before, able to connect in a profound new way with the people around you. Perhaps the feeling it more closely resembles is that which the sociologist Émile Durkheim named *collective effervescence*— the feeling of unity that comes from participating together in some thought or action, when our shared attention enables us to begin to feel together, to share a collective mood or experience. "There can be no society," Durkheim wrote in 1915, "which does not feel the need of upholding and reaffirming at regular intervals the collective sentiments and the collective ideas which make [up] its unity and its personality."

Collective effervescence, as Durkheim imagined it, was a sacred experience, and going to dance has long been likened to going to church. Jamie Principle described the experience of going to the Power Plant as "like going to church, and letting yourself be free without worrying about all the craziness that was happening in the streets and in the world. The music took you away for an amount of hours. You'd get out of the Power Plant club and the sun was shining. It was a totally spiritual kind of thing." If the pilgrimage to the dance is the initiation rite of belonging, then this is that rite's apotheosis—this feeling of collective unity we feel inside as we are caught together in the swirl of the music, the warmth of all these bodies, tearing our hearts open so that we might scatter the fragments like confetti on the strangers around us.

For those who take it, MDMA may amplify this ecstatic feeling of connection with the people around them, but it does not *create* that feeling. Long before the drug's widespread recreational use, the dance floor was already a place of synthesis and connection.

Modern dance music, from its earliest origins, was the result of experiments in combining different sounds and different musical cultures to create beguiling new hybrid forms. This can be traced as far back as the gatherings of enslaved people and free people of colour in New Orleans's Congo Square in the nineteenth century, where African rhythms played on European instruments created the basis for jazz music, perhaps the most influential musical form of the first half of the twentieth century. More than a century later the Black pioneers of house and techno in Chicago and Detroit were also creating new hybrid forms, by combining elements of European electronic music with funk and soul. Paul Gilroy traces this kind of cultural hybridity back to what he calls the "Black Atlantic," a mode of being resulting from centuries of forced migration from Africa to the Americas. This music, defined by its fluidity and heterogeneity, is a kind of radical countercultural response to the certainties of Western modernity, a source of communality and collective identity cre-ated out of diasporic instability and enforced transience. Buried deep in the bone marrow of house and techno is a discourse of belonging—a centripetal force pulling us ever closer together.

At the same time, the dance floor itself may also be thought of as a place designed to disrupt any sense of separation or dis-parity. It does this most obviously by usually being very dark and often streaked by a kaleidoscope of restlessly moving lights. It is a scenography of confusion and disorientation, of intimacy and movement, in which it is rarely clear who anyone is, or even where one body ends and another begins.

The smallest dance floor I have ever danced on was big enough for just two people. It was created by the artist Abi-gail Conway for her performance *On Dancefloors*, for which she invited audience members, one at a time, to choose a song for her and them to dance to.

When I enter, Abigail is at the other end of the room in a white tank top and skinny black jeans, skipping lightly from one foot to the other, arms in the air, head down. She is a good dancer, but not intimidatingly so. Dance is not the content of this performance; it is the medium. And so I close the door and begin an awkward half-skip, half-walk towards the centre of the room, head sort-of nodding, trying to overcome the awkward-ness of dancing completely sober in the middle of the afternoon.

Haze eddies and mirror ball light cascades across the walls as Abigail meets me there in the middle, and by this point I'm finding, if not a rhythm, then at least a way to shed my inhibitions, arms spinning above my head like some wretched sema-phore, and there she is right next to me, waving straight back. The music is too loud to talk and it's too dark to really see each other's faces, and both of these things are important. They create for us an opportunity to try and meet one another in a different way, stripped of the fears and preconceptions that might otherwise define our encounter. Here in this weird micro-club, without say-ing a word to each other, we can find a way to be both vulnerable and ecstatic, to trust one another, to find commonality through an improvised dialogue of adjustments and reflections, her hands moving with my hands, the two of us finding a rhythm together.

In distilling the experience of dancing to its most basic elements—me, her, some music, a dance floor—what Abigail shows me is that empathy can be something our bodies can find even when we can't. That any really good dance floor is an empathy machine—a place where anonymous people of every possible kind can find a shared rhythm, a collective efferves-cence. A kind of understanding that is virtually impossible in any other context. And when we leave the club we carry this understanding with us. It permeates our everyday interactions, a sheen of something, a softening, a reminder of some essential sameness, a gram or two of empathy to rub into our everyday encounters with each other in the occasionally harsh light of the real world. In our tiny club, Abigail and I both lift our fragile arms as high as they will go, and jump together in the almost darkness.

Movement V: A Short Sojourn in the Smoking Area

Here in the smoking area the blissful communality of the interior somehow just about holds together in the smoky half-light, and people's encounters with each other manage to retain some of the easy, anonymous grace of the dance floor, which anyway they carry outside with them on the bottoms of their shoes, in the sweat glistening on their skin, and, circulating invisibly, in their bloodstream. As the music recedes into the background, mixing with the chatter of voices and the sound of cars passing, people move around in search of lighters, rolling paper, some temporary company, heat rising from their bodies like an ascension. They lean against a grubby brick wall in an alleyway that was never intended to be as full of people as it is right now, talking animatedly with strangers about all manner of things no one will remember in five minutes' time. Talking for the sake of talking, for the feeling of connection, wrapping words around other words, feeling the cool air brushing their warm skin, waiting just a few minutes longer before heading inside again.

Let's hear it for the smoking area! That grey patch of nowhere borrowed temporarily from the outside. That slither of yard! That corner of rooftop! That roped-off stretch of pavement! This awkward peninsula of nicotine exile! A new kind of space and a new kind of human encounter forged by the World Health Organisation and a thousand local and national anti-smoking ordinances. Their medical crusade has accidentally created the most beguilingly in-between of spaces! An edgeland of the edgelands, at once inside and yet also outside, a few square metres of otherwise unusable side street or back alley refashioned into a club's most essential gathering place. The place, ironically, where the dance floor stops to catch its breath.

Movement VI: Back to the Centre

We are walking home now, the music still moving in our ears and in our bones. Dawn has risen but the streets are still quiet; there is only the occasional jogger and perhaps a fox slipping quietly out from between two parked cars, alert and suspicious. Soon we will be swallowed again by the city and its familiar daytime rhythms, but for now we walk together in contented silence through the seeming emptiness of the early morning.

No party can last forever, nor should it. Things change, for better and for worse. The edgelands keep shifting and new people set off to find their freedom there.

Perhaps the enforced home-working revolution initiated by the pandemic will mean that once-thriving business districts will soon be as desolate as the industrial areas of the 1970s and 1980s, full of empty glass towers, their blue short-pile carpets fading in the warm sun. Will there be nightclubs on the penthouse floors of otherwise empty skyscrapers? Illegal raves in the derelict shells of franchise dim sum restaurants? The sound of techno drifting across the empty pseudo-public squares of former enterprise zones? Could any building, no matter how banal, if soaked long enough in the right kind of music, feel like it exists at the edge of the known universe?

What will the right kind of music actually be in the future?

Dance music has changed considerably in the last two decades. In the 2000s, US music industry executives made a conscious attempt to rebrand house, techno, and other forms of danceable electronic music under the monolithic new descriptor electronic dance music or EDM, promoting it to a whiter, straighter, mainstream audience by stripping the sound from the radical political context and the marginalised people that nurtured it. No longer primarily a music of the margins, DJs like Skrillex, Calvin Harris, and DeadMau5 can play steroidal EDM beats for hundreds of thousands of people in giant sports stadiums and at major commercial musical festivals, or fly on their own private jets to play exclusive parties for some of the wealthiest people in the world. Calvin Harris alone is purported to be worth $300 million.

At the same time that dance music is drawn towards the centre, the network of spaces that once sustained it is slowly disintegrating. In the 2010s a fifth of all the nightclubs in the UK closed, with many more closures forecast as a consequence of the pandemic. Often it is the small and economically precarious spaces at the margins—queer spaces, for example—that are most vulnerable to disappearance and whose loss is most keenly felt.

COVID-19 has transformed our relationship to dancing at the edgelands in other ways as well. Throughout the pandemic, story after story has emerged of illegal raves in defiance of various lockdowns and the need for social distancing to prevent the spread of the virus. Such events have come from the top and the bottom, organised both by groups of young people recklessly seeking an opportunity to party and by wealthy club promoters and superstar DJs cynically exploiting laxer COVID-19 rules in countries like Mexico and Tanzania to throw exclusive events for wealthy foreign visitors. Perhaps in the end it was always the case that the traits of club culture—hedonism, anti-authoritarianism, a desire for intimacy and proximity, for community in defiance of social norms—might find more dangerous and self-serving manifestations than most of those I have outlined in this chapter.

And yet there are still times when dancing together retains its singular power. In the 2016 film *Raving Iran*, for example, which documents the attempts of Iranian DJs Anoosh Rakizade and Arash Shahram to organise illegal raves in their homeland at the risk of imprisonment or worse. In the film we see them drive out into the middle of the desert and set up their sound system in the soft yellow sand. They play through the night, with no light other than the moon, and then on into a blistering blue morning, smiling beatifically behind their sunglasses as the small rabble of ravers throw their arms ecstatically in the air.

In Berlin it was the fall of the wall that truly initiated the city's now legendary techno scene, as music first nurtured in the West found new devotees and a playground of abandoned Soviet factories and apartment blocks in the East. "The unification of Germany happened on the dance floor," record producer Mark

Reeder recently told the podcast *99% Invisible*. "It didn't happen in politics until much later. Everybody was on the dance floor together, and it didn't matter where you came from, whether you were from the East or the West, how much money you earned, what kind of job you had. Didn't matter."

In Liverpool, as coronavirus restrictions began to relax, five thousand people gathered to dance together in an old warehouse at Bramley-Moore Dock as part of the first legal rave event in the UK in over a year. From my flat in London I watched in wonder the shaky camera-phone videos of the event sent to Beckie and me by our friend Peter. In the videos, it is early and bright and the hall is still more than half empty, but already you can feel people moving together again, the first tingling of that collective effervescence crackling in the air like static electricity as they learn how to be close to one another in a way they haven't for so many months.

Watching this, it is easy to imagine that despite everything—the shifting geography, the evolution of the music, the slow ruination of the club scene itself—dancing together can and will play an important part in overcoming any post-pandemic crisis of intimacy, and in reconnecting us with our communities in the coming years. The ways people find to dance at the edgelands will no doubt look very different in the future, but in my lifetime there has rarely been a moment when I more strongly felt the desire to wrap a building around myself and dance with whoever else happens to be there. To go to church and remind myself, for a few hours, what it feels like to belong to each other.

We are still walking home. The party is over, but I can feel the night still on me. The dance floor persisting stubbornly, defiantly. A memory of a way of being, an idea about how we might meet each other, even if we understand it is only that, an idea. It might be transient, contingent, chemically assisted, and impossible to sustain. A paradox of inclusion through exclusion, of connection through separation. An encounter that appears constantly caught in the process of being reinvented. And yet it does persist, and we carry it with us, as a faint pulse, as a heartbeat.

CHAPTER 7

A GREAT GREEN EMPTINESS AT THE CENTRE OF EVERYTHING

We meet at the railway station, all of us in coats and hats, hands in gloves or thrust deep in our pockets, and from there we walk together towards the park. It's a cold November evening. Bonfire Night, that weirdest and cruellest of English traditions, when we celebrate a failed assassination with fireworks and burning effigies and the whole of this cursed island is wreathed in smoke.

Here in London the air is crisp and the lights of the tower blocks glow white and amber against the dark sky. Someone has a backpack full of red wine, plastic cups and, for some reason, a pair of cheap 3D glasses—the kind that used to be handed out at the cinema during the brief and confusing 3D renaissance of the late 2000s. We hand them round as we walk, enjoying the kaleidoscopic patterns that form like halos around each glowing street light. Budget psychedelia and dark red wine lips. It's 2008 and I am new to this part of the city, allowing myself to

drift along with the crowd as we stroll along the narrow pavement, pausing at traffic lights, zigzagging through a maze of
back alleys and side streets, past rows of wheeled rubbish bins,
parked cars, the steel skeletons of old market stalls.

Around us the city is filled with noise of every kind. Snarled
traffic, raucous drinkers, electric light, and gasoline smog. My
work as an artist has meant that I have spent much of the last
ten years travelling around the world, asking children what they
do and don't like about the towns and cities they live in. Again
and again they have told me the same things. Too much traffic.
Too much noise. Too much violence or too much drinking. They
tell me about problems with pollution. About dirty streets and
dirty rivers. They tell me they don't have enough space. That
there is not enough room for people to live or for children to
play. Not enough nature. Not enough animals. They wish people
were friendlier. They wish there was more to do. They wish for
something more than this. These busy streets. All this concrete
and asphalt. All these engines and all these lights.

And yet here we all are. Caught in the exhaust pipe of modernity. More people live in urban environments than don't. Over
nine million people live in London alone, and on this night it
feels like all of them are out on the town. As we walk, more and
more people appear on the streets around us, thickening into a
crowd as we approach the grand-looking park gates. In the park
people have already started to assemble. You can hear the crack
of beer cans opening and the snippets of excited conversation.
Beneath our feet the grass is soft. We're all here for a good night

out. We're here for the fireworks. We're here for the dancing and the illicit drinking. We're here to feel ourselves blanketed by the bodies of strangers. To offer them friendly smiles and slip them knowing looks. More than anything, we're all here to get away from the city, even if only temporarily. The first fireworks go off and we all crane our heads upwards. The crowd coos as the rocket explodes and little trails of coloured light fizzle above us, our faces briefly illuminated in the darkness.

● ● ●

From the very beginning the city park has been a place to retreat to. The first-ever publicly funded urban park was Birkenhead Park, on Merseyside in the North West of England, which opened on April 5, 1847. Before that there had been many other kinds of urban green space. Cemeteries. Palace gardens. In Europe in the seventeenth and eighteenth centuries there were licentious pleasure gardens, perhaps most famously at Vauxhall in London, where thronging crowds admired the tightrope walkers and the Vegas-style music acts. Preceding even this were the much-mythologised commons, lands upon which ordinary people were free to graze animals but which were technically still owned by the lord of the manor. But Birkenhead Park was something new. An answer to an entirely new social problem— the problem of the modern, industrialised city.

England in this era was in the midst of a decisive transition, from a majority rural to a majority urban population. In 1850 just over 50 per cent of the population of England and Wales lived in urban areas. By the end of the century that figure would be 77 per cent. The North West of England was the birthplace of the Industrial Revolution, and Liverpool was one of the busiest and most important ports anywhere in the world, the so-called "New York of Europe"—a bustling, choking metropolis and the engine room of the British Empire, a place where both new diseases and new ideas arrived and then circulated through the city's overcrowded streets. Birkenhead sat just opposite Liverpool, on the other side of the river Mersey. In 1821 it had been a small village with a population of only a couple of hundred people, but by the middle of the century it was home to over twenty-four thousand. A place every bit as crowded and chaotic as its neighbour on the other side of the river.

Public parks were one solution proposed by the ruling classes to the dangers fermenting in these choked urban communities. A kind of pressure valve, perhaps. Campaigners championed these new spaces as "the lungs of the city" to convey the sanitising effect they hoped this patch of imagined countryside might have on the smoggy, overcrowded streets and their impoverished inhabitants. It was an idea that took off quickly. Parks similar to Birkenhead appeared across the country during this period. There were new parks in industrial cities like Derby, Preston, and Middlesbrough, and in London in 1845 the Crown Estate purchased 218 acres of what was primarily farmland in the working-class East End of the city and transformed them into the city's first public park, Victoria Park—named, predictably enough, for the monarch herself. In Paris, meanwhile, the

Bois de Boulogne, modelled on London's Hyde Park, opened in 1852. New York's Central Park was approved only a year later, in 1853. One of its designers, Frederick Law Olmsted, had visited Birkenhead Park in 1850 and his experience there deeply influenced his plans for Central Park.

Here, then, was a new corollary to all the noise and the dirt and the bodies. Public parks for the working people of a city to retreat to, to soothe their minds and their lungs. A pastoral mirage amidst the churn and the smog. A vision of an older world to soften the hard edges of this new urban reality.

Still today, parks offer something that no other part of the city does. Their geography is so different to the ordered and largely utilitarian urban spaces that we frequent elsewhere. In the streets our encounters are, by necessity, sporadic and fleeting; we catch the eye of a passing stranger, respond apologetically to a request for spare change, or huddle together temporarily out of the rain. Partly this is because so much of our urban space has been given over to cars. Only on special occasions, when the traffic is stopped and people can flood out into their newly reclaimed streets for a carnival or a protest, does the city truly become a site of recreation and meaningful social interaction once again.

A public park, on the other hand, is a geography of openness and possibility. Rather than order and certainty, it is defined by its unreality. It is a stage set built for wandering through. Beneath it run railway lines and sewage tunnels. Beyond the rows of trees obscuring its outer boundaries, it stops as neatly and suddenly as the edge of a painting. It is an imaginary space designed to offer its users a temporary sort of freedom, a retreat from some of the harsher realities of the city and the programmatic lives the vast majority of us are obliged to live there.

A park is somewhere decidedly *other*. Somewhere greener and wilder, closer to the natural world. When I walk through the park by my house, if I half-close my eyes I can transport myself from the furious noise of the city to an idealised version of the English countryside, open fields fringed by oak and chestnut trees, interrupted by little ponds on which ducks and swans float with the unhurried gentleness of a Beatrix Potter story. Whether you are escaping from the stresses of your job, the noise of your apartment block, or the suffocating emptiness of your bank account, in this theatre of possibility the green grass unfolds before you like a vast empty stage.

This pastoral otherness to the rest of the city makes a public park a space defined not by any specific use we are supposed to make of it, but rather by its lack of specificity. Sidewalks and underpasses and even public squares are places designed to encourage very specific kinds of use—narrow pavements to walk along, benches to sit on, statues to admire, stairs to climb. Activities that transgress from these uses—such as skateboarding or napping or simply loitering in the wrong place—are viewed with suspicion and even hostility. A park, on the other hand, is intended to be only what the clogged streets cannot be. Here, in this uniquely open and shared public space, people seek out a freedom they cannot find elsewhere in the city.

• • •

Marcus Garvey Park is twenty acres of grass and trees orientated around a steep stone outcrop on the border between Harlem and East Harlem in New York City. Before it was Marcus Garvey Park, it was Mount Morris Park, and before that it was Mount Morris Square, which officially opened to the public in 1840, right at the beginning of that decade of desperate urban space clearing and park building. From the very beginning Mount Morris Square had hosted musical performances, but there is nothing in its long history quite like the summer of 1969, when the third annual Harlem Cultural Festival transformed it into an ocean of bodies moving in eddies and waves to the sounds of Nina Simone, B. B. King, the Staple Singers, and Sly and the Family Stone.

In Questlove's Oscar-winning documentary about the Harlem Cultural Festival, *Summer of Soul*, the sky is a deep, empty blue and if you hold your face close enough to the television screen you might still feel the heat of that New York summer. Out of the streets they spilled, arriving at the park like water condensing on a cool glass. First a handful, and then more, and then more. Until a crowd had formed under that empty blue sky. Then the music started, and everyone danced together in the sunshine.

In the film, festival organiser Tony Lawrence is standing on his stage in a cream-coloured suit and a soft pink shirt and tie. Around and beneath him are so many people that the park itself disappears. People have climbed into the trees for a better view, children have scrambled over the steep rocks. A boy in a giant sombrero nods his head in time to the music. A woman in a white chequered shirt sways to the beat. "All I remember," says the actor and producer Musa Jackson, recalling being at the festival as a kid, "is going to this amazing concert in the park and there was just a sea of Black people . . . as far as I could see it was just Black people. This was the first time I'd seen so many of us." It was, he says, "incredible," and as he does so his voice rises in astonishment, as if seeing all those faces again and for the first time. All those people, all those faces, familiar and unfamiliar at the same time.

To some extent, every city park is an empty space. Or at least, every park is empty in relation to the urban space around it. And one thing about that emptiness, something so simple it seems ridiculous to even point it out, is that you can gather a lot of people there. More people than anywhere else in a busy city.

The summer of 1969 was hot and fraught in Harlem. Questlove interviews a festivalgoer called Darryl Lewis who tells him he always associated the summer with violence and anxiety. Martin Luther King Jr. had been assassinated only a year earlier, and Malcom X three years before that. White supremacy was attempting to choke the life out of the civil rights movement, and the Black community was divided as to how to respond, whether with violence or non-violence. But here that community was gathered as one, able to meet each other's eyes, to share this single open space. To be a part of a crowd. As Musa Jackson describes, simply recognising how many people there were out there in the city was a joyful feeling. To understand in a very tangible way how big your community is. How many people there are like you. "Beautiful, beautiful women, beautiful men," he says. "It was like seeing royalty." On stage the Reverend Jesse Jackson leads the crowd in a chant. "I am Black," he says, and the crowd sing it back. "I am beautiful," he says, and they say, "I am proud."

This is what it can mean to be a part of a crowd. To feel that sense of belonging. That collectivity. To dance or sing together, en masse, as a way of consolidating a collective identity. This is especially true when you are part of a culture or a community that has been marginalised or diminished in your own city. Seeing yourself and other people like you come together as one— feeling yourself to be a part of something larger than you—is an empowering experience. It is one of the reasons why events like Carnival and Pride continue to be such important civic gatherings. As the writer Barbara Ehrenreich has argued, these rituals of collective joy have always been an essential part of human society, right back to our earliest days.

Parks are one of the few places in the density of a modern urban environment where such gatherings are still possible. Even a park as small as Marcus Garvey can be a gathering place for thirty thousand people. Nowhere else in the city can those thirty thousand people come together in the same way. Large, open, traffic-free, parks are also familiar spaces—easily recognisable and a good meeting point, free to access and, crucially, convenient to get to. Most residents of Harlem and Spanish Harlem didn't have to ride a subway, or even a bus, to the Harlem Cultural Festival. They didn't need a car, as did most of the people who attended the Woodstock Festival the summer before.

For this reason, parks play an essential role in the life of a modern city. They are a vital outlet for the expression of our collective joy. A place where we can come to look at each other and be together, to recognise the scale of the community we are a part of—the sheer number of bodies that make up the people we live amongst. In an environment of fracture and fragmentation they can be places of consolidation and solidarity. A place to retreat to and regather. A place from which to begin.

● ● ●

What is it that begins there, in that expanse of green? What does the crowd desire when it gathers? Collective joy, certainly, but sometimes also collective discontent.

As well as singing and dancing in the summer sunshine, parks have long been places where people gather for more explicit acts of social transformation. Every protest march I have ever attended has begun in a park. My own local park, Victoria Park, has long been the site of political gatherings, protests, even riots. In 1978, for example, eighty thousand people from all across the country descended on the park for a free open-air concert organised by the groups Rock Against Racism and the Anti-Nazi League as a protest against the rising tide of fascism in East London. Or, some forty years earlier in the same park, when Oswald Mosley's Blackshirts were thrown out of the East End by a coalition of anti-fascists made up of local trade unionists, communists, anarchists, British Jews, and gangsters. My grandmother still remembers looking out at the park from her cousin's window as a little girl and seeing the police horses circling on the green grass.

Elsewhere, parks have regularly been a site where larger protest movements have either begun or been consolidated. In Hibiya Park in Tokyo, for example, where riots began in 1905 that shook the foundations of Japanese society; or in Grant Park in Chicago during the Democratic National Convention in 1968, when people gathered to protest the Vietnam War; or in Gezi Park in Istanbul in 2013, when a sit-in was held that initiated a period of unrest that nearly brought down the regime of President Recep Tayyip Erdoğan.

No wonder so many regimes have considered parks dangerous, refusing to build them or trying in one way or another to diminish their power. This is not a tendency seen only in explicitly autocratic regimes. There are certainly crass and obvious ways to get rid of parks—bulldozering over them to replace them with a shopping mall and a barracks, for example, as President Erdoğan had planned to do to Gezi Park. But there are other more insidious ways as well, through allowing the inequities of the market to slowly chip away at the promise of freedom offered by a truly open, truly public urban space.

On a damp spring morning in my local park, I can stand in the same spot where the Clash's Joe Strummer ripped into "White Riot" and the crowd moved like an ocean in a storm. It's basically just a green field now, but it still retains the possibility of a reoccurrence. Some rebel spirit glitters beneath the surface like fragments of broken glass trodden into the mud.

Come the summer, however, I won't be allowed to stand here. By then this area of the park will be taken over by the commercial festival producer AEG for their annual All Points East Festival (£68.55 plus booking fee for a one-day pass, or £132.95 for the VIP package). Bands will again be playing here to a packed crowd, but attendance will be strictly limited and tightly policed. A three-metre-high steel perimeter fence will snake its way across the park, rendering over a third of its 218 acres completely inaccessible to the general public. A temporary gated enclosure built literally on top of the people's park as a means for a cash-strapped Tower Hamlets borough council to generate the funds they need to maintain it.

It may not seem particularly significant that, for a couple of weeks each summer, a portion of the park is appropriated in this way. It might even be a good trade-off for this vast public resource to remain clean and well-looked-after for the other eleven months of the year. And yet I think this festival and others like it represent an existential threat to the beautiful promise of the public park. It is a first incursion of the economic and political logic that governs the rest of the city into this space that for so many years has managed to remain separate from them.

Just on the other side of the River Lea from Victoria Park is another park. It too is fawningly named for the queen who reigned over its creation. The Queen Elizabeth Olympic Park was opened following the Olympics of 2012—a spectacular new green space in London's East End, twice the size of Victoria Park, dotted with landmark stadiums from the 2012 Games, surrounded by tech startups, expensive new cultural spaces, and tower after tower of new-build apartments. This park, however, belongs not to the city itself but to the London Legacy Development Corporation, who tightly monitor its use, both by limiting the events and gatherings that can take place there and through a discreet array of closed-circuit TV cameras and a proactive on-site security team.

Rather than empty green spaces whose use can be negotiated by the park's users, the park is made up largely of pathways and facilities that demand that the user interact with them in a very specific and limited way. You walk along the walkways, cycle on the cycle track, exercise in the exercise zone. Its tiny ornamental lawns are broken up by landscaping and a maze of gravelled pathways. The way the park is used doesn't vary with the seasons, because there really is only one way it can be used: politely and obediently. This is not a space of spontaneity and negotiation. It is a leisure facility for the residents of the apartments that surround it.

What it lacks more than anything is openness. Ambiguity.

Perhaps even that particular quality of emptiness that I think of as the essence of any good park. The kind of emptiness that invites speculation and possibility, that brings thousands of bodies skipping across a city in search of another world. Either the makers of this new park don't trust that we will figure out our own way of making use of all this space, or they fear what the consequences might be were we to do so.

If the Olympic Park is a vision of the future of parks, I think it is a bleak one. It is the product of an authoritarian turn in late capitalism, a desire to limit and control ordinary people by designing out opportunities for transgression, dissent, and even the kind of productive social tension that might lead to new bonds of empathy and solidarity between otherwise disparate communities and social groups. Instead we are invited to enjoy spaces of ordered comfort and frictionless consumption—a real world that is as navigable and controlled as your iPhone operating system.

It is a reminder also that not all parks are created equal. That sometimes it is the messiness and the awkwardness, that excess of freedom, that makes a place special.

• • •

And perhaps also, the fact that one of the freedoms you have in a public park, when compared to other urban spaces, is the freedom to get away with a little bit of mild law-breaking.

As a teenager I did all my adolescent law-breaking in two places—at friends' houses when their parents were away, and in our local parks. We knew, for example, the best place in the park by our school to sneak off in between lessons and smoke weed, even though none of us really knew how to smoke weed. And we also knew the one newsagent's in town that would sell alcohol to anyone, no matter how young they looked, and we would go there to buy as many cheap bottles of vodka lemonade as we could afford and drink them ostentatiously on Parker's Piece, the flat square of grass just around the corner. In the daytime no one paid us much notice, and at night we could slink out into the darkness of the interior, where the street lights illuminating the pathways could not reach us. No matter how cold or rainy it got we would drink until we were drunk enough to tell each other the things we couldn't when we were sober. Drunk enough to pick fights we wouldn't follow through on with the kids from Parkside school. Drunk enough to link arms and fall down on the wet grass just to be close to one another.

When, a few years ago, I travelled to rural British Columbia to interview local high school kids about their school playing field, it was reassuring to hear that this green space played the same role for them some two decades later and an ocean away. They told us about spontaneous night-time gatherings, illicit drinking, woozy games of moonlight football, new couples disappearing into the shadows by the edge of the park. Everyone figuring themselves out in the only space in town available to them. The closest thing they had to freedom.

For teenagers, this period of gleeful transgression is normally a phase. A brief time in your life when you have decided to begin experimenting with the adult world in dark corners where the actual adults cannot see you. For some people, however, this freedom to pursue their desires is never granted, and so the relative privacy and anonymity of the park remains a necessary retreat from the rest of the city.

In *Dancer from the Dance*, Andrew Holleran's seminal novel of gay life in New York in the 1970s, the characters retreat from the stifling heat of their apartment to sit in the park until the early hours of the morning. "The park was used by two classes of people," he writes. "The first group came early to walk their dogs before going to sleep in the air-conditioned bedrooms of their townhouses . . . they were usually gone by midnight, and then, like ghosts, like gremlins, the derelicts, the faggots, drunks, and freaks moved in." Here the park becomes a kind of refuge. A home for dispossessed people and their fugitive desires, at least until dawn broke and the denizens of the respectable world reclaimed this precious green space for themselves. "Until that moment, however, it was the perfect place to rub the itchy sore of lust—the perfect cave in which to lick your wounds—for half the lamps did not work, and in the shadows of those trees, it was very, very dark."

Darkness brings with it certain kinds of freedom, but it also carries inherent dangers. Parks after dark have long been associated with a fear of violence. I remember the feeling I had walking through Battersea Park in London once very late at night as each set of lights flanking the path in front of me flicked off one by one, like a scene from a horror movie, plunging me into an absolute darkness unlike anything I had experienced on the streets of the city. Even in the daytime the emptiness of certain parks, not to mention their reputation, is enough that many of my friends, my queer and femme-presenting friends in particular, would never think of venturing through them alone.

Yet if you are someone who has little choice but to seek the refuge of a park after dark, such dangers became a grimly necessary part of your day-to-day experience. In his book *Queer London*, Matt Houlbrook describes the litany of assaults and robberies that gay men were subjected to in parks throughout the early part of the twentieth century as they sought out the kind of sexual encounters that were prohibited in almost every other context. And yet, despite this danger, he suggests the parks became a place of "communality and affirmation." One of the few places in the city in which gay men could meet and interact openly with other gay men. Over time, cruising established itself as a completely distinct kind of social encounter. An invisible world existing at the margins of the known city. And in the darkness of Haywards Heath or Clapham Common, that same sense of belonging was being forged that had so electrified the sunbaked audience at the Harlem Culture Festival. The feeling of being a part of something. Of knowing you are not alone.

• • •

The thing that sustained these hidden communities was the etiquette of cruising itself—the delicate language of looks and gestures through which gay men made themselves known to each other in public: the request for a cigarette or a light, the particular way a look is returned, a private knowledge glowing white hot. In this way the park "became the necessary locale of tenuous moments of privacy." A private world emerging out of the freedom afforded by this most public of spaces.

This delicate balance between the public and the private enables each of us to create for ourselves our own shared community. And each of these communities is in its own way a private community, with its own rules and its own etiquette, yet all of them exist together in the gregarious public space of the park, rubbing up against one another, even overlapping.

In 2020 and 2021, when the COVID-19 pandemic meant London's many shops, bars, and restaurants were closed for months on end and new rules were instituted that limited our ability to meet inside, the city's parks became an ever more essential public resource. Thousands spilled out of cramped apartments into the parks as virtually the only space outside of their houses that they were allowed to go. It was a reminder of how little outdoor space most people in this densely packed city have access to, but also of how lucky we are to have such beautiful, expansive, and well-cared-for public parks.

I returned again and again to Victoria Park, running in the early morning, walking the dog, sitting and reading on my own, taking a stroll with a friend or enjoying a socially distanced picnic. Despite the constantly shifting rules that sometimes prohibited sitting down on benches—or, for a brief and surreal period, outlawed any stopping at all—Victoria Park largely remained a place of possibility and hope in a time of restricted freedoms.

And when the summer of 2020 arrived, a walk through the park in hazy afternoon sunshine revealed how many people in East London were celebrating their birthdays at exactly the same time, each in their own distinctive way. There were the groups of thirty-somethings gathered on a picnic blanket, drinking fizzy wine accompanied by posh crisps and supermarket dips, bunting strung up from a nearby tree and the celebrant's age spelt out in giant foil-balloon letters. There were the children's birthdays, with presents and party games and children chasing each other in circles whilst their parents chatted quietly on the sidelines. There was at least one large group of twenty-somethings sprawled out together on the grass, taking drugs in the sunshine with an exhilarating lack of discretion, snorting bumps of coke off each other's fingers whilst they sunbathed and danced and listened to music. There were the big, sophisticated Afro-Caribbean birthdays, with barbecues, gazebos, and trestle tables full of homemade food. There was the guy who brought a whole sound system down to the park, blasting out old garage tracks loud enough for everyone to dance along. There was the birthday party that took the form of a softball tournament; another an entire sports day, with sack race, egg and spoon, friends wheelbarrowing each other along a running track marked in cheap blue ribbon. There was the birthday that was just four people eating pizzas in the shade. And there was my friend John's birthday: no picnic, no music, but drinking takeaway pints in plastic cups, laughing at old jokes, keeping an eye on our errant dog, enjoying the sunshine and the brief semblance of normality.

Each of these groups was enjoying its own private birthday, and yet we were all also experiencing these birthdays together, not just when we had to run over to borrow a lighter or apologise for the intrusion of a dog or a child or a Frisbee, but because we were out here in public celebrating in sight of one another, collectively. The park transformed into one giant birthday party. A single shared encounter, like a song with too many verses, each sung to its own beautiful, peculiar tune.

This is one version of the park's particular balancing of public and private. When we were all there, separately and together, doing the same thing. Dancing or cruising or singing "Happy Birthday." And then there are other times. Times when the park becomes a more dissonant place and our activities there no longer rhyme.

• • •

Beckie and I got our dog four years ago, an eleven-week-old miniature poodle we named Sausage. Beckie carried him home in the palms of her cupped hands. He is sleeping beside me as I type this, curled up on a footstool like an oversized croissant. When he struts through the park he has the poise of a ballet dancer, and when he stares at you his dark eyes are two empty holes to the bottom of the universe. He screams like a banshee at the doorbell and the neighbour's cat and, more often than we would like, at other dogs, especially spaniels, who inspire in him an irritation that is occasionally breathtaking. Of course I love him completely.

In a study at the University of Warwick, psychologists attempted to measure the impact that a dog has on our sociability. For ten days a researcher recorded every human encounter she had as part of her usual daily routine: five days on her own, and the other five accompanied by a young adult Labrador. On her own, the experimenter had three encounters with strangers. On the five days she was accompanied by the dog, she had sixty-five. One could easily conclude from this simply that a dog is a good icebreaker, a way for humans to overcome social reticence. But this arrogantly and unfairly reduces a living, breathing companion to an object of curiosity, like a table ornament or an outlandish hat. Dogs are actors with their own wilful desires, fixations, and fears. Their own way of being in the world. They are experts in tactility and proximity, oblivious to the conventions of human social etiquette. They drag us into unexpected encounters with strangers, their unprejudiced, unembarrassed curiosity forcing us to initiate conversations with people we might otherwise dismiss or ignore. Through sheer force of will, dogs draw us closer to the people around us.

Despite being only four years old and a maniac, Sausage has taught me how to be better at being in the world. Each morning, come rain or shine, we take each other for a walk around the park by my house. Sausage likes people and seems convinced that his mission in life is to meet all of them. In the park he pursues this task diligently, navigating his way through thickets of trees and across great expanses of grass in search of other dogs and their companion humans, darting through the low banks of mist towards any distant smudge of activity, looking back often to check I am still following.

In this dance of sociability, I always follow where he leads. He pulls me into encounters with every possible kind of person. We stand at a distance of a few metres from each other, this stranger and I, hands in pockets, watching our dogs circle each other carefully, until eventually we begin to speak. We start with something innocuous—some comment about the weather, perhaps, or a polite enquiry about the names and ages of the dogs currently wrestling each other across the damp grass. From here the conversation squirms its way into talk of our plans for the rest of the day, or for the weekend, about the films we love or the football teams we support; stories about our lives, our jobs, the illnesses we have or worry we might have, the relative cleanliness of parks in the UK and America. In the park I have had conversations with strangers about house moves and miscarriages, about soup kitchens and Lebanese history, about the many and varied failings of Tottenham Hotspur, about London's acid house scene in the 1980s, about loneliness, about the fear we all felt during the pandemic, how we longed for it to be over and worried it might never be.

Out of those conversations have blossomed genuine friendships. Through Sausage I have become part of a community I wasn't even aware existed before. A hidden network of dog owners—the residents of their own private world. And unlike many of the other micro-communities I am a part of in the rest of the city—those determined by work or social life or the apartment block I live in—this Dogland is almost as heterogenous as the city itself, made up of people of every age, economic status, social background, political affiliation, religion. It is a community whose threads were woven together solely by the inscrutable whims of animal affection.

There is Kris, who speaks with a mouth full of thick Minnesota vowels and dreams of moving to live in Scotland by the sea. There is John, who drives a taxi and is forever just about managing his two huge English bull terriers, holding their long leads like the reins of a runaway train of horses. There is Chloe, who as a teenager was part of a cult riot-grrrl group, and Connor, whose job in film is so secret he can't tell me anything about it. At Halloween people and dogs dress up in costume and meet in the spitting rain on the back field by the park café. Sausage wears a pair of bat wings. Someone brings a flask of hot cider and we drink it out of plastic cups. We talk together in small groups, floating in and out of each other's orbit in pursuit of our respective companions, making sure they aren't getting into any more trouble than usual. The dogs bicker and run, darting in and out of our feet, binding us together in the grey morning.

• • •

Any park is an ecosystem. In it these small communities are able to germinate, each making space for itself amidst the others. And like any ecosystem, each park is slightly different—made up of its own peculiar network of social groups and niche interests, determined by the neighbouring communities, the geography of the park, the interests of the era we are living through. Groups congregate and disperse at different times of the day, like some cacophonous symphony. Life in a thousand movements.

In my own local park, for example, on a Saturday at the height of summer, the day begins just before dawn as the park wardens make their rounds, their hazard lights flashing in the soft light as they unlock each gate in turn, enabling the city to begin drifting in, an array of little communities, each moving to its own rhythm, following its own private schedule.

First there are the ravers, the club kids, the all-night partiers, yesterday's last stragglers stumbling through the dawn with the night still crackling around them. They sit in the centre of the otherwise empty park enjoying the stillness of the early morning, like picnickers at the end of the world, drinking a beer or snorting lines of white powder off the back of someone's phone. Willing the day not to begin just yet.

Then come the dog walkers—the earliest of them, at least, like my friend Sheila, who takes her dogs Rascal and Scallywag out at the same time each morning, following the same loop around the path, shouting at them to stop picking up scraps of discarded rubbish or eating bread that's been left out for the birds. The dog walkers will continue to arrive in a steady trickle for the rest of the day, gathering in informal clusters in the open lawns where the dogs love to run. They drink coffees and exchange pleasantries, complaining bitterly about the amount of rubbish or the speed the cyclists ride at. They know each other as much by the names and character of their dogs as they do each other, and they are all fundamentally happy with this arrangement.

Then there are the runners. They are men and women, old and young, some bundled up in old jogging bottoms and sweat-shirts whilst others are in tiny shorts and club vests. There are fast runners and slow runners. Runners with dogs and runners with strollers. Runners who prefer to stick to the hard asphalt and those who run through the soft grass. Runners who go clockwise and those who go anticlockwise. Sometimes there are pairs of runners or a little train of people or a tightly packed cluster, and just occasionally I see one particular phalanx of serious-looking men in serious-looking running gear who like to occupy nearly the entire width of the path as if the world belonged only to them. Increasingly there are races, formal and informal, where runners gather in larger numbers, swapping times and stories, complaints about injuries, and aspirations for future races. But even when they run alone, there is a recognition of their shared identity. An understanding that they are all small pieces of each other's mornings. Those brief sparks of recognition. Faces that pass each other every day.

Later on, the footballers arrive, marking out their territory with plastic cones and temporary goals. There are the club footballers, the junior footballers, the women's footballers, the teams with shirts sponsored by local businesses, the five-year-olds whose coach coaxes them gently from the sidelines whilst parents clap and cheer every small success, the lads in secondhand bibs who organise their own games in the spaces between official matches. There are the cricketers in the summer months, white lines etched into the grass to mark their borrowed corner of the collective space. There are the ultimate Frisbee players, the softballers, the touch rugby players. There are the skateboarders in the skate park, forty-year-olds in worn jeans moving with nonchalant ease and eight-year-olds in helmets and knee-pads practising a first trick as their nervous parents watch on. The roller skaters lay out their little orange cones on the path and slalom through them. The anglers stake out their spots by the pond. A yoga class materialises under a nearby tree. By the end of the day, as dusk arrives, they all slowly drift away, the picnickers pack up almost all their rubbish, the footballers take their cones away, the dog walkers do a last circuit. The runners are the last to leave, their breathing still audible through the gloom, just as the wardens make their final rounds, locking each gate as night draws in.

These are just the things I can see happening. There are undoubtedly more. More hidden communities, each with their own rhythms and their own routines, their own private languages. Birdwatchers. Metal detectorists. Alcoholics. Bodybuilders. Remote-control car enthusiasts. Conspiracy theorists. Psychogeographers. Communists. Recreational walkers. Evangelical Christians. All of them gathered here alongside, and occasionally on top of, one another. Held by the park in that delicate state between public and private, visible and invisible. Just about managing to live together in this way.

But living together is not always easy. Especially on those warm summer days when thousands of people emerge from the overcrowded streets. On such days the park strains to contain the many purposes people have for it, layers of meaning accruing on its busy lawns, colliding with one another. An over-tossed Frisbee skids into a circle of picnickers. An excited dog spooks a nervous toddler, who runs to their father in tears. The booming bass line churning from a portable sound system disturbs the concentration of someone quietly reading. A cyclist in a hurry cuts across a jogger who screams at them to slow down.

Such encounters, micro-incursions into each other's lives, are what the sociologist Richard Sennett might call "social friction." For Sennett, the experience of such friction is an essential part of the life of a city. Cities are by their nature fraught and crooked places, "full of contradictions and jagged edges." They are where a society's inequalities and injustices are most tangible, where its prejudices and its stresses are most amplified. If humanity itself is flawed and fractured, then the city is where those fractures are most profoundly tested. The challenge of urban life is to be able to sit with this complexity, however hard that may sometimes be.

● ● ●

Two stories of times when this precarious balance of public and private appeared to collapse:

In 2009, in Jubilee Park on London's South Bank, I was involved in creating a street game for a summer festival. Promoted by the Southbank Centre, the piece encouraged players

215

to dress in one of three colours and meet outside the Royal Festival Hall, freezing for two minutes and then moving in a series of improvised patterns towards the middle of the park, where we had prepared as a finale a giant version of the game we call grandmother's footsteps (also known as red light, green light) led by a performer in a giant papier-mâché grandmother's head.

As the people playing the game started to move in fits and starts across grass, dozens of other people—including many of the local teenagers hanging out and drinking in the sunshine—tried to join in. These new people did not know the rules, had not received the pre-event briefing emailed to players the previous day; they were in fact intruders in a private game. Or, perhaps more accurately, we had appropriated the public space they were using for a game they were not invited to.

In delighted exhilaration they rushed at Grandma. Responding instinctively to the danger posed to the performer braced inside the oversized costume, we formed a cordon; arms linked, we pressed into the crowd, forcing them backwards. Behind me I could hear another supervisor using a loudhailer to encourage these new players to disperse. This was not the kind of play we had anticipated, and not the role we thought we would find ourselves playing.

In 2020 a Black man called Christian Cooper was birdwatching in an area of Central Park in New York known as the Ramble, a popular spot for birdwatchers. Whilst there, he noticed a white woman, Amy Cooper, who had allowed her dog off its leash despite the park bylaws prohibiting her to do so in this area of the park.

This is the kind of minor disagreement that happens a thousand times a day in a park as big as Central Park. One person contravening the rules or disrupting someone else's enjoyment of the day—driving too fast on their bike, leaving out bread in an area where they shouldn't, thumping a football right into a group of picnickers—and then being scolded for doing so by someone else. Normally it is our responsibility to resolve these private disagreements between ourselves. It is part of the work of being together in this public space.

Amy Cooper, however, responded to being reprimanded by this fellow park user by calling the police and falsely claiming he was threatening her life. In her call to the police, she attempted to exploit the country's long history of anti-Black racism to cast Christian Cooper's polite confrontation with her as a malicious intrusion. An invasion of a space that, by implication, should have belonged exclusively to her. In doing so she threatened not only his right to be in the park, but his very right to exist at all. Fortunately in this instance, things did not escalate beyond this initial altercation, and when mobile phone footage of the incident began circulating online there was widespread public sympathy for the plight of a birdwatcher who was simply trying to uphold the park bylaws and found himself in a potentially life-threatening situation. In the end, Amy Cooper lost her job at a major investment firm whilst Christian Cooper recently began hosting his own birdwatching show on National Geographic TV.

We are all occasionally interlopers in each other's lives. This is part of the complexity that Sennett and others ask us to sit with when we move about the world. The danger of these moments is that we might, out of carelessness or anger or fear, believe that our version of reality should take precedence over anyone else's, and begin to act accordingly. Such actions threaten to spoil the principles that underpin the very idea of a public park, the beautiful promise that this space could and should belong equally to everyone.

• • •

Navigating the complexity of this space can be difficult. It requires confronting our own privileges and prejudices. Recognising how we are different from the people around us—and the hard work that will be involved in overcoming those differences. This is also why these spaces are good and necessary. But, as Richard Sennett argues, increasingly the design of cities aims to eliminate this discomfort. Trends in urban design are moving more and more towards closed rather than open environments. Towards being insulated from difference rather than confronted by it.

No kind of urban space better exemplifies this trend than the gated community; in many ways it is the complete opposite of a public park. The gated community is the pre-eminent architectural form of our age, on the rise across the world—from residential communities with their own private security to vast suburban business campuses; all of them aggressively private spaces accessible only by an exclusive group of users. These are spaces that Sennett argues are "in the city but not of it"; keeping the messy complexity of reality hidden on the other side of a wall.

The same might be said of so-called pseudo-public spaces like shopping malls and privately owned and managed squares and parks, such as the Queen Elizabeth Olympic Park or the vast new Hudson Yards complex in Manhattan, where a facsimile of the open, messy reality of the city is quietly policed by private security staff who enforce adherence to a set of inscrutable rules and prohibitions that intentionally exclude any undesirable elements, be they communities of homeless people, gangs of teenagers, or indeed anyone who fails to conform to a particular model of acceptable attire and behaviour.

The aim of such urban planning is to enable wealthy citizens to move through the city with frictionless ease; living, working, and socialising within designated spaces shared only by people similar to themselves, largely insulated from the complexity of the world around them. Here the problem of cities is not something to be confronted or negotiated, but rather to be avoided entirely.

Public parks might be thought of as an antidote to this kind of thinking. They are spaces of openness and complexity. Synchronous spaces where different uses and meanings overlap and intersect. Where the public and the private coexist and sometimes conflict with one another. This is especially true for parks that exist at the borders between different neighbourhoods and

communities, thus encouraging people from different backgrounds to encounter each other. This is a category of park that
Frederick Law Olmsted, the designer of Central Park, called a
"gregarious space." The encounters we have in these gregarious
spaces may be illuminating, they may teach us something new
about the people living around us, but by design they may also
be difficult, requiring us to reckon with privilege, difference, and
the limits of our understanding of those things.

It is no accident that when I spend time in the park by my
house at the height of summer, when the sun blisters the grass
and sweat and laughter and birdsong and weed smoke swirl in
the air, London feels most alive to me. It is when the city feels
really present, existing suddenly not as an agglomeration of
buildings, a network of roads, an abstract civic entity, but as a
teeming mass of people, currents of movement and desire, faces
and voices and *souls* maybe—maybe even souls—connecting in
ways that are infinite and unknowable and, yes, wonderful to me.

• • •

The fireworks are over and we make our slow way back towards
the exit. The crowd is splitting apart. Some are heading towards
the nearest bar, others back to their cars to begin the journey
home. Children swirl glow sticks around and around in front of
them, making spinning wheels of light appear in the darkness. I
can feel the crunch of beer cans beneath my feet. In a few hours,
as dawn breaks, the park wardens will be out again, collecting
all the detritus, loading it into the backs of their trucks. Sweep-

ing the night away. I think about all the people it takes to keep a park running. A whole barely visible civic infrastructure to sustain this imaginary square of bucolic countryside.

A public park feels like a miracle at the best of times. The last truly open space in our diminished public realm. All these gloriously unproductive green acres, occupying vast amounts of expensive real estate in the middle of busy towns and cities. All this effort just so we can come and play, hang out, kick a ball around, have a picnic. Or worse, drink and take drugs and fuck, start a protest, start a riot. Attempt to bring down the government.

The problems associated with urban space are not going anywhere. Indeed, many are getting worse. According to the Brookings Institute, over the last twenty years income and wealth inequality have been rising in practically every advanced economy, particularly sharply in the US. Meanwhile the UN Refugee Agency warned in 2021 that "ninety percent of refugees under UNHCR's mandate, and 70 percent of people displaced within their home countries by conflict and violence, come from countries on the front lines of the climate emergency." The number of climate refugees will only increase over the next thirty years, with many of those people likely to end up settling in already dense and unequal urban environments. The UN predicts that by 2050, two-thirds of the world's population will live in cities. This will necessitate an unprecedented level of urban density and all the concomitant issues that arise as a consequence— noise, pollution, housing costs, access to essential resources like schools and hospitals. Our towns and cities are fraught places and only likely to become more fraught in the coming years.

Parks are not and have never been the definitive solution to these problems. But they are a remedy. A place of refuge and connection. We still think of parks as the lungs of the city and see their value in ecological terms. They clean the air and cool the city. They are oases of green where we can run and walk amidst so much suffocating urban sprawl.

But to me, the real oxygen they provide us is the range of encounters they foster—from the collective euphoria of a crowd of thousands to the knotty discomfort of a private disagreement. Each of these meetings can help us to better understand our place in the world and our relationship to the people around us. They are vast green organs, breathing empathy and solidarity back out into the fractured metropolis.

CHAPTER 8

SPACE TO DREAM

The Lights Are About to Dim

In the movie theatre the lights are about to dim.

Audience members trickle in, carrying giant bags of popcorn and Coca-Colas in oversized paper cups. On the screen they are playing an advert for a Volkswagen hatchback, but no one is paying any attention. Instead they whisper to their neighbour, check their messages one last time. Nothing much is really happening. It is like an aeroplane before take-off, which is to say it is just an unusually shaped room full of people talking. Filling time before take-off.

If nightclubs are spaces that belong to the edgelands, the cinema in contrast has always been connected to the city centre. It was born out of the smoky metropolises of the late nineteenth century. An invention forged in crucibles of electric light.

In the Claude Monet painting *Boulevard des Capucines*, Paris is a flurry of people and movement beneath a bright winter sky. It was here, on this street, on December 28, 1895, that the Lumière brothers first presented their *cinématographe* to a paying audience in the basement of the Café Grand. They gasped as the hand crank was turned and pictures began dancing on the wall in front of them. Soon this device and others like it were everywhere—Paris, London, Berlin, New York. The latest and most spectacular in a long line of mechanical parlour tricks that had dazzled the music halls and the fairgrounds. No other art form could reflect the riotous discontinuity of the modern metropolis quite like the cinema, all whirring mechanics, noise, perpetual motion. It spoke to ordinary people's experience, a frantic new entertainment for a frantic new century. A magic lantern made vividly, sometimes frighteningly, alive.

Ever since then, a visit to the cinema has been a journey to the centre of everything. A journey that takes us through busy city-centre streets, past crowded bars and restaurants or the brightly lit windows of popular chain stores, onwards towards the sugary smell of the concession stand. And when we arrive, we tumble inside with modern life still ringing in our ears. We are here. The middle of the city. The centre of the culture. The place that everyone wants to be.

And then something unusual happens. The lights dim and all of this melts away. The cinema auditorium, this space full of people eating and drinking and whispering to their neighbours, reveals itself to have been not an aeroplane, but a rocket ship.

A place of darkness and noise. A machine for faster-than-light travel. A square-shaped hole in reality. In our air-conditioned isolation we watch imaginary worlds appear on the screen in front of us—faraway planets or distant eras, exotic and unfamiliar locations, or just our own world made beguilingly strange through the image-making apparatus of the cinema. Suddenly everything outside the auditorium is a thousand miles away and we are all just floating in space.

These Rows of Faces

Here we all are then, floating in space. "This loving darkness," as the writer Annette Kuhn described it. It is half past ten in the morning on an ordinary Thursday in June and the biggest cinema in London is absolutely full. On the screen, Tom Cruise is flying fighter jets. This man I have never met but whose face I have known all my life is taking off his sunglasses again, riding his classic motorcycle, laughing his maniacal movie star laugh, each of his beautiful teeth the size of my whole hand. Outside it is grey, but in here it is always that golden hour just before dusk.

Who are all these people who have travelled miles from their homes to the centre of London to watch Tom Cruise first thing on a Thursday morning? I look around and the answer is, seemingly, everyone. Families with young children. Teenagers. Older couples. Lone thirty-something men breathing through sobs before the opening credits have even finished. This movie has already made a billion dollars at the global box office. In every part of the world, people of every kind have gathered to watch this film. It is playing at rooftop cinemas in Athens, at the AMC Classic in Des Moines, at the US Navy's Downtown Lyceum theatre in Guantánamo Bay, and here at the BFI IMAX just by Waterloo Bridge.

We are here to be entertained. To see the anxieties of our age reflected back to us by beautiful strangers. To give the kids something to do for a couple of hours. To impress a first date with our good taste. Or just to be near to other people. These rows of faces illuminated by the reflected glow of the pictures on the screen in front of us.

Cinema prides itself on being for everyone. The pre-eminent mass public leisure activity of the twentieth century—cheap, accessible, and open all day. The doors of the cinema are almost always open, and we are all invited to gather there. Rich and poor, old and young. There is room enough for everyone. It is a place of mass entertainment, of *popular* culture. A busy social space in which a broad range of people can feel welcome and safe. Even large groups of teenagers, viewed with fear and suspicion in almost every other public environment, are welcomed and trusted—research by geographer Phil Hubbard at an Odeon cinema in Nottingham has demonstrated that adults find the presence of gangs of teenagers significantly less threatening in the cinema than they do in other areas of the city.

My own teenage years were spent roaming dizzily around our local multiplex, jacked up on fizzy cola bottles from the pick-and-mix stand, strategising for the best way to sneak the youngest of our friends into movies they were not yet old enough to go to. The cinema was one of the few places we were given licence to roam, safely ensconced in the familiarity of its bright blue carpets, watched over by the loving eyes of our favourite Hollywood stars.

The cinema is and always has been a unique proposition. It is a venue with the potential to bring together disparate parts of a community and place them in intimate proximity with one another. All those bodies squeezed into all those rows of seats. All those different faces, staring up at the screen together.

And yet, from nearly the very beginning, cinema has also been in the process of splitting apart. Stratifying and segmenting, separating itself into an infinity of genres, each more arcane and specific than the last. Science fiction movies. Western movies. Gangster movies. Disaster movies. Zombie movies. Pornographic movies. Big-budget musicals. Sword-and-sandals epics. Swashbucklers. Biopics. Romcoms. Melodramas. Animation. Documentaries. Film noir. Grindcore. Blaxploitation. Ozploitation. K-horror. J-horror. Bollywood. Nollywood. Wuxia. Spaghetti Western. Giallo. Italian neo-realism. New French Extremity. Mumblecore. New York fish-out-of-water comedies from the 1980s. Paranoid thrillers from the 1970s. Talking-animal movies. Time-loop movies. Movies in which a team of plucky underdogs have to learn the importance of friendship on their unlikely journey to becoming champions. Movies where the vastness of space slowly sends someone insane.

And whilst some movie theatres are for everyone, many are

not. There are the scuzzy B-movie palaces where kids would gather, away from the expectations and conventions of the adult world, to eat sickly-sweet treats and watch blood splatter across the screen. To feel the illicit thrill of something danger-ous and unknown and belonging entirely to them. The same is true of the horror fans in their black T-shirts and Doc Martens crammed into the ballroom of the Radisson Park Inn to watch low-budget haunted-house movies at the Horror-on-Sea fes-tival in Southend-on-Sea, or the serious-looking middle-aged couples watching Apichatpong Weerasethakul's *Memoria* at the Institute of Contemporary Arts in central London. It is true of the *Star Wars* fans queueing outside the Odeon Leicester Square for hours on end and the Marvel fans filmed roaring in ecstasy at the climax of *Avengers: Infinity War*.

It is definitely also true of the fish-netted *Rocky Horror Picture Show* fans I once spent a wild night with, dressed in nothing but a borrowed pair of white tights and a blazer, eyeliner crudely scrawled below each eye, hair sprayed into an ineffectual quiff. I felt so conspicuous on the way there, I sheepishly pulled on a pair of jeans for the taxi ride, but once we arrived at the cinema any inhibitions melted into the crowd as we sang along to every line, throwing rice at the screen, the movie itself just a score that we were all playing along to. The order of service in a ritual of belonging and becoming: A place to hold tight to each other, to shore ourselves amongst these liberated bodies against the crueller, colder parts of the outside world. This was cinema not as mass entertainment, but its opposite, a place of intimate and

228

secluded community. A private universe with its own rules and its own dress code.

Like the city itself, the cinema is an exercise in community. A place where the great swirling mass of humanity is broken up and organised, siphoned into precariously overlapping groups, all ready to figure something out about themselves and each other in the time they have together before the credits start rolling and they go their separate ways.

Being an Audience

The audience has gathered, the lights have dimmed, and the film begins to play. And then what?

The straightforward answer is that they sit there and watch the film together. But whilst this is technically true, it also feels somehow completely inadequate. Something else is *happening* in that darkness. Call it what you like—liveness, active spectatorship, the magic of the movie theatre—we are doing more than simply sitting together in silence, staring at the moving pictures. How then can we begin to describe all the other things this act of collective watching encompasses? How can we name the other moving parts of this encounter—the stuff happening quietly, even illicitly, in the background whilst the film blazes away noisily on the screen in front of us?

Back in 2009, I was asked to create a one-off performance for an event at the Institute of Contemporary Arts (ICA) in London. I proposed to use one of their two cinema spaces to present the first known re-enactment of a performance called *Moveyhouse*, a "happening" by the artist Claes Oldenburg that had taken place at the Film-Makers Cinematheque in the Forty-first Street Theatre in New York in 1965. Audience members arrived at that performance under the impression they were there for a screening of a new experimental film, only to find themselves stood in the aisle, watching instead the bank of cinema seats where Oldenburg's performers played the role of cinema patrons—laughing, drinking, eating popcorn, occasionally shouting at the screen, the whole thing wreathed in cigarette smoke and the bright white light of the whirring projector. This was cinema without the cinema—"everything in attendance but the actual event," as Oldenburg himself described it—all the myriad actions and interactions that occur out of sight in the cinema placed suddenly on display, like lifting up a log to study the insect life teeming beneath it.

The ICA would not allow me to use either of their cinemas for my version of *Moveyhouse*. Not wanting to disrupt their regular programming, they instead offered me the use of an empty studio space on the other side of the building which they said they would set up like a cinema: folding chairs arranged in neat rows in front of a portable projection screen. But this would not do. The spirit of cinema did not haunt this empty studio. I decided to abandon my first idea and, as a kind of tongue-in-cheek protest, rather than re-enacting Claes Oldenburg's *Moveyhouse* I chose instead to make an entirely new performance in which the live audience would re-enact everything that was happening a few hundred metres away in the cinema I had been refused the use of.

On the night itself an audience of around forty people arrived at the ICA for my version of *Moveyhouse*. They sat in their make-believe movie theatre and watched as descriptions of everything happening in the cinema just down the hall were projected onto the screen in front of them in the form of a stream of text messages from a group of collaborators I had smuggled into the theatre for this explicit purpose:

> Just sat down. Couple whispering.

> People walking in late are quite annoying.
> Fortunately I am one of them.

> Someone coughed but managed to do it quietly
> about 6 rows back.

> The main character, who looks a lot like Al Pacino,
> falling over in a dance routine elicits minor laughter.

> A guy three rows back has rested his leg on the
> empty chair in front of him.

> Just got told to stop texting by security.

> Everyone shifts. That was intense.

As these descriptions appeared on the screen, the people in the room began responding. Coughs and whispers and ripples of laughter. On the screen, my interlopers reported that someone had gone to the toilet, so in our make-believe theatre someone also stood up and left. Another volunteer appointed themselves a security guard and started patrolling our little square of seats, waving a flashlight and occasionally demanding that people stop texting. Popcorn was eaten and occasionally thrown. Couples whispered. People rested their legs on the seats in front of them. Slowly, out of the smokeless air, a cinema audience began to appear in front of me.

Watching the banal micro-drama of the cinema come to life was an education in what it is that is actually going on in a cinema. Suddenly I could see the patterns and the rhythms, the way laughter moved through the air like perfume, how excitement built and inhibitions diminished. Even in the absence of a film itself, my audience knew what it meant to play the role of a cinema audience. They implicitly understood the shape of this encounter and what it required of them. They were all of them fluent in the language of moviegoing.

I could see how the people in the audience communicated wordlessly with each other—a language of coughs and shushes and whoops and giggles. It was a volatile, unstable thing, this audience; dormant one moment, then feverish the next. One moment a single collective entity, so many mouths laughing or yawning or screaming in unison, before fragmenting back into a room full of separate individuals and their private interactions— little whispers to a neighbour or looks exchanged along a single row of seats.

On the screen, the text said everybody gasped, and so everybody gasped, and for a moment at least we were all breathing together.

The Shush

Make too much noise at an Alamo Drafthouse cinema and an usher will seek you out in your seat and hand you a little white card. The card is there to inform the recipient, in neat sanserif lettering, to "respect the movie going experience and refrain from talking and texting. Continued talking or texting will result in you being asked to leave without a refund." Although talking and texting are emphasised in print, in practice you can be handed one of these little white cards for anything that another guest considers to be disruptive. On Twitter recently, the writer and director Claire Downs shared that she had been handed one for "laughing at inappropriate times" during a screening of Baz Lurhmann's *Elvis*.

At the Alamo Drafthouse, strictly enforced cinema etiquette is part of the brand. As well as the prohibition on disruptive noise of any kind, there are no latecomers and no unaccompanied minors, the only exception being fifteen-to-seventeen-year-olds who have submitted a special application demonstrating their understanding of the theatre's values and policies. As the cinema's founder, Tim League, has written, "When we adopted our strict no talking policy back in 1997, we knew we were going to alienate some of our patrons. That was the plan. If you can't change your behavior and be quiet (or unilluminated) during a movie, then we don't want you at our venue." At the Alamo there are no teenagers illicitly kissing in the back row, no well-timed heckles, no unexpected laughter floating through the auditorium like leaves caught on the breeze. There is only cinema, bathing in a pool of quiet and admiring concentration.

The Alamo Drafthouse did not invent cinema etiquette. There have been hundreds of sets of guidelines advising cinema patrons on how to behave, written by everyone from *Reader's Digest* to Debrett's, the official social coaches of the British aristocracy. All these rules tend to boil down to that most seemingly reasonable of things: consideration for the people around you. Watching a movie in a busy theatre is a test of our capacity to take care. To rein in our individual desires for the sake of the collective experience. Perhaps a set of agreed-upon rules can help remind us how to do so.

But how do we agree? How do we know what the right way to behave is? How we choose to watch a movie is contingent on the context and the company. The idea of a right way of watching a movie is as absurd as the idea of there being a right way to walk through the park or eat a slice of pizza. Setting your rules in stone is the easy way out, a means of creating another gated community where otherwise there would occasionally be tension and the difficult work of recognising the complexities of place, community, and culture that always inform how people behave. It is a way of avoiding the need for each audience to figure out what kind of audience it wants to be.

It also means the end of the shush, that most weird and powerful of audience weapons. A little splinter of unvarnished opinion. A sibilant grenade tossed up in the air, hanging there in the darkness for a few seconds before detonating with awkward silence, muffled laughter, or barely suppressed offence. Everyone knows what a shush means. You feel it in your bones. It is the moment where something breaks, in which an audience stops being a collective thing and everyone invisibly picks a side. Now suddenly we are all in wordless conversation with one another. A disagreement is in the process of being resolved.

Sometimes such disagreements are resolved quickly. One person recognises themselves as out of step with the people around them and either accepts the majority decision or leaves. They are too noisy and need to be quiet, or they realise their call for silence was misjudged and they grudgingly put up with the noise and watch the film.

Sometimes, however, a shush is just the beginning of something. The opening jab in an all-out brawl. In the Wayans brothers' horror parody *Scary Movie*, for example, when Regina Hall's noisy Black cinemagoer is stabbed to death by a pack of irritated white audience members during a screening of *Shakespeare in Love*, the cartoonish excess of the scene belying the darker commentary playing right there on the surface. Or in the 2021 film *The Lost Daughter*, when a prickly English academic played by Olivia Colman is watching a film in a makeshift cinema on a Greek holiday island, only to be interrupted by a gang of local boys who take over the screening. Her furious attempts to get them to be quiet achieve nothing, highlighting the suffocating isolation that swirls around her like a fog.

Such incidents are not about one or more people breaking the rules. Instead they speak to larger social and cultural differences that cannot easily be overcome. In doing so they reaffirm the in-betweenness of the cinema auditorium. A place that is both inside and outside, that is inescapably connected to the politics of the world outside even as it strives to distance itself from them. A place where our attempts to imagine new kinds of reality are constantly being undermined by the divisions in this one.

The Kiss

Most of the audience are too distracted watching the movie to notice the occasional click of the shutter opening and closing. I do not know exactly what the film is—some 3D spectacle that requires them all to be wearing little cardboard glasses with coloured lenses. They are staring straight ahead, eyes fixed on the screen. Almost all of them, at least.

There is one young couple sitting right in the middle of the auditorium who are not watching. She has kicked off her shoes and rests her bare feet on the seat in front of her, toes curled around its wooden frame. He leans right over in his seat, arms wrapped around her, the fingers of his hand slipping under the back of her top. Her arm rests on his shoulder. They are kissing. A long, passionate kiss. Their mouths closed and their faces pressed tightly against one another, as if they are trying to keep something trapped in the space between them. There is the sound of a mechanical click, but they do not appear to notice.

The girl is not wearing any 3D glasses, unlike the elderly lady with the handbag slightly farther down her row, or the man in the suit directly behind her. She makes no pretence of watching the film. Neither does the boy she is with. Sometimes it's not the film you go to the movies for, or the strangers around you. Sometimes it is the darkness.

The photographer uses an infrared film with an invisible flash so as not to alert the audience to his presence. Weegee has been surreptitiously taking these photographs for a few years now, perhaps as an extension of the fascination with spectators increasingly apparent in his better-known work as a crime photographer on the streets of New York. Perhaps it is also a response to his own burgeoning celebrity—a discomfort with his own visibility at the crime scenes that made his name. Here in the darkness of the movie theatre he can be anonymous, even invisible, again.

The darkness of a cinema is a special kind of darkness. A permissive, promiscuous darkness. Even as late as the 1970s, when Denys Lasdun was designing London's new National Theatre, theatre buildings were understood to be, at least in part, a space of social display. People attending the theatre did so in the knowledge that they were there to see and be seen. Cinemas have always been different. The cheap tickets and overwhelming air of informality presented an opportunity to disappear for a while. This has long made cinemas a good place for romantic encounters. As Weegee's photos demonstrate, even in a crowded cinema, a couple could weave a private space for themselves out of the darkness, somewhere in which to hold each other close.

If anything, as cinemas have become less popular, their usefulness as places for illicit encounters has only increased. An almost-empty auditorium is an even better place in which to hide away from prying eyes. In 2013 I was invited to curate a festival of UK-made performance work in Bangkok. To host this miniature festival, we chose as our venue a cinema in Siam Square called the Scala, a beautiful thousand-seat 1960s Art Deco wonder that sat amidst the modern shopping malls like some forgotten prince or a Fellini film left to yellow in the sun, its cavernous lobby empty except for the ageing ushers in their canary-yellow suit jackets. The young Thai artists we worked with on our programme were delighted when we said the festival would be taking place at the Scala—they told us it was much loved by young people in the city as a place you could take a date you didn't want to be seen with, knowing you could kiss away to your hearts content in its vast auditorium safe in the knowledge that no one who mattered would be there to see you. Whilst the modern multiplexes in the nearby shopping malls were all full of people enjoying the latest Hollywood blockbusters, in the Scala there was nothing but empty seats and a handful of young teenagers kissing passionately in the shadows at the back of the room. In its decaying darkness they were both a short metro ride from their houses and a thousand miles away from anyone.

Who knows if any of the people that Weegee captured were

there with someone they shouldn't have been. Using the cinema's disconnection from the outside world to do things they wouldn't be allowed to do there. "Do you feel guilty at all?" Celia Johnson asks Trevor Howard as they take their seats in the front row of the balcony in the film *Brief Encounter*. Emblazoned on the screen in front of them is the name of the movie: FLAMES OF PASSION. She sits stiffly in her seat. "Why should I feel guilty?" replies Trevor Howard, turning to look at her. "How awfully nice you are." *Brief Encounter* is a romance of glances and things left unsaid, two people who cannot be together almost getting together and then not doing so. The story of a kiss that doesn't happen. This encounter in the cinema is as intimate as they will ever get. A secret moment stolen away from the reality of their ordinary lives. That notorious British stiffness melts just enough for them to lean towards one another and laugh, whilst the flames of passion rage on in the background.

Sometimes simply being together in that loving darkness is enough. Giving yourselves the freedom to sit for a while unseen by the world. Much more so than the characters in *Brief Encounter*, we today live in an era of relentless visibility. What a relief, then, it is to be plunged into two hours of comforting nothingness. To establish, even if only temporarily, a relationship to the people around you that is not predicated on the act of looking and being looked at.

One of my most memorable experiences in a cinema involved not being able to see anything at all. An entirely unromantic encounter that was nonetheless as intimate as anything I have experienced in these strange dark rooms. In 2015 the artist Britt Hatzius created a performance for cinemas that required its audience to enter the auditorium and put on a blindfold before the film had even started playing. A few moments after I had done so, I heard the sound of children entering the auditorium and sitting down in the row behind me. Into my hand was carefully placed the end of a thin cardboard trumpet which I was encouraged to hold against my ear. Through it I could hear a child's voice whispering descriptions of the film that was playing in front of us. Their voice stumbled and stuttered, constructing precarious towers of words in an attempt to describe everything they could see happening. "There is a ball, a white ball. It might be an egg. Maybe it's an egg. Yes, yes, it's definitely an egg." They took such care in trying to tell me what was happening. Little images appeared in my mind, floating there for a moment before bursting like soap bubbles. After half an hour or so, the voice said goodbye, their job done. By the time we removed our blindfolds, they were gone and the film was already over.

This experience reminded me that a cinema is an imaginative space whether you are watching a film or not. All that darkness, that empty space, is designed to be filled by the imaginary. Usually it is an imaginary determined for us by the filmmakers, but we can also use that space to do our own imagining. To imagine new relationships between people. Intimate acts we are exploring for the first time, illicit relationships that would scandalise people in our everyday lives, or new ways for strangers to listen to and care for one another. A collaborative remaking of our relationship with each other.

I like to imagine that is what is happening in Weegee's photograph. A kiss as an imaginative act. Arms brushing against arms for maybe the first time. Tender and firm all at the same time. That lightness in the stomach. Goose bumps prickling the skin. A new world conjured in the darkness, unbeknownst to the people sitting nearby. A reality of their own creation, to be carried back out into the real world, or just left there in the cinema with the spilt popcorn and the discarded 3D glasses.

The Laugh

The Cameo cinema in Edinburgh is cinema for cinema lovers, with all the make-believe pomp and circumstance of cinema itself, from the illuminated letters on the exterior awning, to the ornate columns lining the auditorium, to the plush velvet curtain that retracts to reveal the screen. But on this night no one was loving cinema all that much. As the film dribbled on into its second hour, the audience members scattered across the largely empty auditorium were growing restless, wondering idly how much longer was left and if it was really worth staying till the end. Smartphones didn't yet exist, but if they had, people would have been tweeting their disdain, texting friends to make plans for dinner.

It was around this time that the laugh happened. Another implausible plot point. Another vacant stare from Jonathan Rhys

Meyers. Scarlett Johansson picking another awkward line of dialogue out of her teeth like a stray piece of spinach. Whatever the
moment was, it triggered a snigger in the mean part of my chest,
and when I sniggered, so did my friends next to me, and the
people in the row in front. Little peals of laughter falling through
the darkness like fresh snow, landing on the shoulders of our fellow audience members as the actors smouldered on obliviously.
Soon the rest of the audience were laughing too. Nearly all of
them. Each implausible new plot twist greeted by fresh laugher.
This errant thriller transformed into Woody Allen's best comedy
for years.

"[L]aughter allows the audience to become aware of itself."
So said the French film critic André Bazin. And it's true: the
laugh was the moment we became more than an audience. It
was the moment we became aware of each other as people with
desires and expectations, people with opinions who were all
stuck together watching the same dumb movie.

From the very beginning, some people have been very suspicious of cinema and its influence on the masses. What kind of
meaningful social interaction can occur when we're all sitting
in the dark, not speaking to one another, our attention entirely
focused on the mechanical spectacle in front of us? Very little,
these critics would argue. In their reading cinema is a dead
space, all the more so in the age of the multiplex, when films
are products produced by vast media conglomerates. "The task
is consumption," writes the sociologist Zygmunt Bauman, "and
consumption is an utterly, irremediably individual sensation. The

crowds filling cathedrals of consumption are gatherings, not congregation, clusters, not squads, aggregates, not totalities. However crowded they might be, there is nothing collective in these
places of collective consumption." All those disembodied heads
shoving overpriced popcorn into their gaping jaws, slurping on a
supersized Coca-Cola and laughing and laughing and laughing.

But I want to believe there is more to it than that. The film
theorist Julian Hanich calls laughter in the movie theatre a way
of constructing a public space. Laughter is a language through
which we can share our feelings with each other, a language
particularly well suited to the cinema—a way of speaking about
the film without needing to talk over it. And so, when first I
laugh and then you laugh and then everyone else laughs, we are
establishing a common ground, a space of shared understanding. "Laughter thus not only has a communicative function ('we
share the information that we find this scene funny') but also
a collective-awareness function ('we are now aware that in this
public space we find this funny together')." Through laughter
the cinema becomes a place of discourse. A public conversation about what we each find funny or not funny. In this space
our laughter has the power to change things. Indeed, it has the
power to change us.

In 2013 and 2014 a group of researchers at the Max Planck
Institute for Chemistry in Mainz, Germany, conducted a study
that measured the chemical composition of the air in a cinema
auditorium during various screenings. What they discovered
was that throughout each movie, especially during moments of

humour and suspense, the audience were broadcasting chemicals out into the air as part of their reaction to the events on the screen. Using prior studies that have demonstrated that humans possess the ability to detect such chemicals through smell, and that doing so can alter our perception of human faces, they posited that "the chemical accompaniment generated by the audience has the potential to alter the viewer's perception of a film."

Whatever is happening here is more complicated than passive consumption. We are literally breathing each other in, absorbing the feelings of the strangers around us. What we see on the screen is in part a function of this chemical connection. Our view of the world subtly altered simply by being in proximity to these other bodies and their different ways of seeing. Their fear and their laughter becoming part of us.

The Scream

The audience squirm uncomfortably in their seats, coiling themselves around the armrest or each other, seeking respite in some new arrangement of hands and legs and arms but never finding it. Mouths gape and everyone's eyes are opened very wide, watching the screen like it's an intruder standing in the corner of the room. The man in the baseball cap brings his hand to his mouth. He holds it there, fingers clasped around his jaw. The woman next to him in the leather jacket mutters a few words to herself. Her hands are hidden under her coat, which rests on her knees like a blanket. Everyone in the cinema is waiting—

massaging their temples, chewing on sleeves, gripping the hand of a loved one—and the wait seems unbearable.

And then finally the scream arrives. It moves through the audience like a pane of glass cracking. Arms bracing. Heads ducking. Shoulders tensing. Everyone briefly lifted off the ground by the sheer volume of heartbeats now filling the air.

When they land again the spell is temporarily broken. They laugh, or shake their heads, and look across at their neighbour. The man in the baseball cap and the lady in the leather jacket turn to look at each other. The cinema is dark, but the night vision camera is as reliable as ever. Their eyes meet. A look that is equal parts disbelief and reassurance. *We are both still here. We are both as terrified as each other. It's not over yet, but it will be over. We'll get through this together.*

It was the low-budget 2007 found-footage horror movie *Paranormal Activity* that first popularised the trick of using night vision footage of test screen audiences as a way of marketing scary movies. In its official trailer, fragments of scenes from the actual film are interspersed with black-and-white shots of audiences recoiling in terror and delight, pinned to their seats or clinging to the person next to them for support. For anyone watching it was clear what this film wanted you to know about it. More than the plot or the special effects or the names of the actors or the director, this film wanted you to know that it was scary. This film was intended to scare you, and if you were to go and watch it, then scared is what you would be. This, it turned out, was exactly what people wanted. To this date, films in the

Paranormal Activity franchise have made nearly a billion dollars at the global box office.

Movies have always been scary. From their very earliest days, being scary has been one of the things they are most known for. If cinema has a founding myth, it is the story of the first screening of the Lumière brothers film *L'arrivée d'un train en gare de La Ciotat*—how the audience scattered in panic, believing that what they could see on the screen was a real steam train rushing towards them. It's unclear the extent to which this story is actually true, but its persistence in the popular imagination is itself illustrative. I think we like this story because it helps us to believe that cinema is, and always has been, a place where you go to sit in the dark and watch the most dangerous things you can imagine come hurtling out of the screen towards you.

Ever since then, cinemas have promoted themselves as places where we can go to be *safely* afraid. Places where the imaginary feels dangerously close. Where our worst fears can become hauntingly real. Monsters loom menacingly in the dark—vampires, werewolves, zombies, aliens, ghosts, serial killers, creepy children, mask-wearing bogeymen, wronged high schoolers, psychopathic doppelgangers, clowns, demons, haunted dolls, even the devil himself. Places of comfort and familiarity are visited by ever more baroque horrors. A masked figure stalks a suburban neighbourhood. A shadow appears behind the shower curtain. The school is full of murderers. The gas station is run by cannibals. There's someone under the bed. There's someone on the back seat. There's a face in the mirror. The soundtrack crashes and everybody shrieks in unison.

Cinemas are just far enough removed from our real lives that these monsters can safely exist there, but close enough still that we worry they might follow us home. The most notorious horror movies—*The Exorcist*, *The Blair Witch Project*, *The Texas Chainsaw Massacre*, *Antichrist*—all arrived in cinemas trailing stories of audience members fainting in the aisles, vomiting, being carried out on stretchers to waiting ambulances. A spectre haunts such movies, as if they are somehow cursed. As if the horror could not possibly be contained by the thin skin of the cinema screen. By the end of ninety minutes, it will have got us all.

But the truth is that it's never the film that gets us. It is, after all, just shadows on the wall. The truth is that the fear was already here in the room. We brought it into the cinema ourselves. The call is always coming from inside the building. The scary film simply gives us licence to release that fear. It reflects our fear back to us and we all respond on cue, together. To allow ourselves to be scared in this way, to hold each other, to scream as one, is thrilling and cathartic. Where else are you allowed to admit how scared you are and to recognise that same fear in the people around you? Where else can you let it all out? A whole room screaming in terror.

This, too, is something the producers of *Paranormal Activity* understood—we go to the cinema not just to be scared by the film, but to be scared by and with each other.

You can watch those night vision videos of *Paranormal Activity* audiences on YouTube—notice the way, after each jump scare, people's first response is to look over at their neighbour to check their reaction. To share a look of acknowledgement. To admit to themselves that they are just as scared. The legendary film critic Pauline Kael once described the allure of the theatrical experience as being about "sharing this terror, feeling the safety of others around you, being able to laugh and talk together about how frightened you were as you leave." I think this is true of all films, not just horror movies. The world is terrifying, but in here we can be terrified together. The train comes hurtling towards us, but we are ready to meet it. We hold each other tightly until the moment the lights come up, and then we all go our separate ways.

A Final Round of Applause

At the end of the movie the screen turns black and the music soars.

Somewhere at the back of the theatre, someone begins clapping. Their friends join in. Soon this flurry of applause is tumbling through the auditorium and we are caught up in it. I am clapping. We are all clapping. The film is over and we are celebrating the film. Three cheers for the film! These ten thousand feet of celluloid! These three hundred gigabytes of data! Perhaps we are cheering the projectionist for another job well done. Perhaps we are hoping that if we cheer loudly enough, the film's stars will hear us from across the Atlantic, a faint ringing like tinnitus in their perfect ears. Or perhaps we are just cheering for us—for the great job we did of being an audience.

It may not seem like we did much at all, all of us sat here together in this almost-silence. Encounters in the cinema are rarely as difficult or as intimate or as euphoric as some of the others covered in this book. Nonetheless, I think they are just as important.

The cinema is a place where the real and the imaginary meet and the encounters that we have there are shaped by this. There is just enough darkness and just enough make-believe that we can test new bonds of sociability. A kiss shared or a hand held can be an invitation to imagine new possibilities for your relationship with someone you love, or someone you want to love. A shared laugh or a shared scream or even a collective round of applause are all ways of recognising ourselves in other people. Of feeling that most important thing: belonging.

Perhaps more than anything, being in the cinema is a reminder of the value of simply being together, experiencing something communally and how doing so changes the thing that we are experiencing—makes it scarier or less scary or funnier or dumber or more brilliant. It is a reminder of the collective power we have. Of our capacity to change things.

This is what we will lose if cinemas continue to slip towards obsolescence. Not the movies themselves—they will probably always exist—but the experience of being a moviegoer. Over the decade prior to the pandemic, cinema attendance had been in gentle decline across the US and Europe as streaming services made accessing films at home easier and easier. Then the pandemic arrived and they tumbled over a cliff. For months on end, cinemas were shut completely or only open in a limited way. Big film studios like Warner Brothers, Paramount, and Disney either shunted their big releases to unspecified future dates or shuttled them onto streaming services. Cinema itself has since made a slight return, but many individual theatres did not make it, and many people still refuse to go back. Perhaps they never will. The alternatives are cheaper, safer, and so much more convenient.

Is this the beginning of the end? The final gruesome death scene? Or just the moment in the third act when everything seems lost before the comeback we all hoped was coming. If the movies have taught me anything, it is to hope for a happy ending. I believe we can fall in love with going to the cinema again. It can be affordable, accessible—a place for the young and the old, the rich and the poor, to gather to watch flickering pictures come to life in the dark. Our air-conditioned rocket to the moon right in the middle of the high street. We will all go to the movies together again. And at the end of the film when the screen goes black and the music soars, we will stand up and every one of us cheer.

THE END

CHAPTER 9

THE SIMPLE PLEASURE OF
HOLDING HANDS

There is a photograph by the artist Briony Campbell that I have been thinking about a lot recently. It is a close-up of a hospital bed. Briony holds her dad's hand, now so pale it is almost translucent, as if soon he will simply fade away like a painting bleaching in the sun. His hand rests on hers, and she presses down gently with her thumb on the back of his hand. She holds him. He holds on. Her strength and his frailty bound together in a simple gesture of love.

The photograph is part of a series called *The Dad Project*, from 2009, through which Briony documented in intimate detail her father's illness and eventual death from cancer. The series is a chronicle of grief and disappearance, a slow and painful act of letting go amidst the banal detritus of hospital wards and sick beds. They are hard images to look at, softened by moments of kindness, humour, and hope. Fleeting memories of the lives

Briony and her family used to live that puncture the darkness like fireworks in the night sky.

Whenever I see this photograph, I am never quite prepared for it.

When I saw it again recently, the first thing I thought about were all the people over the last few years who never got to hold this hand. All those unseen deaths in COVID-19 wards and care homes, all those unheld hands. The goodbyes that happened through glass windows or Zoom screens, and the goodbyes that never happened at all.

What does the absence of touch do to the way people love? How do they experience loss or pain or fear without a hand to hold? What happens when the human instinct to reach out for comfort and reassurance is denied by the cruel circumstances of a global pandemic?

And what happens next? Will the afterlife of all this fear and disease be a reluctance to hold hands in the same way? Will the precarious network of associations we have woven around this simple gesture over hundreds of years shift and reform once more? Will we retreat towards the limits of our own bodies again, hands buried firmly in pockets or wrapped in gloves, offering the world little more than the occasional nod of acknowledgement, a smile of sympathy? Will there be a time when we no longer hold anyone at all?

Could it ever really come to this? It seems more likely the instinct to reach out and hold on will persist, even if for a while it is marbled by this memory of disease and infection. After all, at this stage we have been holding hands for so long.

• • •

On YouTube you can watch amateur footage of sea otters holding hands, floating on their backs, half-submerged in greenish-blue aquarium water, drifting in lazy circles with their stubby legs pointing straight up in the air and their arms locked stiffly together. At one point they separate and begin to float away from one another, only for the tank's artificial currents to bring them back together again, their arms reaching out to pull each other close, oblivious to the chorus of *ah*s from the watching humans, their eyes wrinkled shut and their hands tightly clasped, like toddlers pretending to be asleep. As of the time of writing, this video has been watched twenty-two million times.

The outrageous cuteness of these otters makes it easy for us to project our human associations onto this little quirk of animal behaviour. To see in them the things we want to believe about ourselves. But really these tenderly held hands are, more than anything, a utilitarian tactic, a way for breeding pairs to sleep without losing their mate, enabling them to rest whilst still floating out on the open ocean, well away from any predators like us waiting by the shore. The same behaviour has not been observed in river otters, who sleep on dry land and float much lower in the water.

Chimpanzees have also been observed holding hands, primarily as a form of conflict resolution. A means of soothing their animosity and fear after a fight has broken out. Although the way they hold hands is very different to the otters' behaviour, it arguably serves the same essential purpose, helping them stay together in an unpredictable and frequently hostile world.

Holding hands is hardwired in our animal brains. When we are physically connected to another person in this way, it soothes us. In 2006 psychologists at the University of Virginia and the University of Wisconsin-Madison used neuroimaging technology to explore the ways in which the human brain responded differently to threatening stimuli when the subject was holding someone's hand and when they weren't. They found that holding a loved one's hand significantly reduced activity in the parts of the brain associated with emotional and behavioural threat response. Even holding hands with a complete stranger "conferred a basic level of regulatory influence on the neural response to threat cues." In other words, holding hands made people less anxious in stressful situations, a comfort blanket thrown over the most jittery parts of our brains just when we need it the most.

When I was a student I had a part-time job as a ghost tour guide through the subterranean passageways that spread out beneath Edinburgh's Old Town. Of the many companies that offered similar tours, ours was probably the most shamelessly trashy and macabre. We were dressed by our boss in shabby black cloaks and party-shop top hats, told to make sure it was a B-movie thriller of a tour, designed primarily to scare the half-drunk tourists who would gather by our hand-painted red and black billboard on the Royal Mile, illustrated with screaming faces and lettering dripping with blood. The tour began in a one-room torture museum and ended in a pub, and in between I would lead giggling groups of visitors through a series of incrementally darker rooms until we ended in almost total darkness, illuminated only by the faint beam of my cheap battery-powered torch.

At which point the atmosphere would inevitably change. Whether you believe in ghosts or not, that amount of darkness is intimidating, the cold damp air disconcertingly tomb-like, everything smelling of neglect and decay. The giggling would subside. You could sense bravado dissolving, and then, in the near dark, I would watch the outlines of hands reaching quietly out towards their neighbours, fingers wrapping around fingers, bodies shuffling closer to one another. Often people ended up holding hands with whoever was closest, whether they knew them or not, grasping instinctively for comfort, for human con-tact, the same reassurance we have been seeking our whole lives—that we are not about to wake up and find ourselves all alone in the darkness.

These are the first kinds of hands we hold and the ones we always return to. The hands that ensure we stay safe. That pre-vent us from disappearing. The hands that reassure us when we are afraid, that comfort us when we are sad. These are the hands that teach us how to do things we aren't sure we can do, that guide us across a road or help us balance on a wall. These are the hands that pull us woozily through a packed crowd of dancing bodies, the hands that we squeeze when we know how much it's about to hurt. These are the held hands that guide us gently into a world full of adult dangers and adult problems and these are the kind of held hands we reach for instinctively when that adult world leaves us feeling small again and uncertain, alone in a darkness we could have anticipated was coming but which nonetheless we find ourselves completely unprepared for.

• • •

At primary school we played football on the field behind the school unless the ground was wet, in which case we stayed on the concrete playground and played Red Rover.

Red Rover is a game that involves two teams of children standing in rows opposite one another, two parallel chains of held hands facing off across a few square metres of playground. Each team in turn would have the opportunity to call out the name of someone on the opposing team. That person would then run as fast as they could at the children in front of them, hoping to break one of the links in the chain. If they were successful, they returned to their own side; if they failed, they joined the opposing team.

There was always a lot of debate about the arrangement of the chain. A constant note of frantic bickering in pursuit of the strongest possible combination—big holding small, strong holding weak, the bravest holding the most afraid. This was one of the only times when boys and girls could hold each other's hands without embarrassment. After all, this mattered more than gossip and slander. This was Red Rover. I remember how it felt to stand there, strung out across the rain-slick playground, each child testing the strength of their bond with the person next to them, nervous hands squeezing each other so tightly their fingertips glow from the effort, bracing in anticipation of the weight of a small body ploughing into our thin blockade.

Red Rover is an irresponsible game. An obvious kind of battle-by-proxy that rewards strength and fortitude and demands callous strategising about the weakest links in your own and your enemies' ranks. It is a relic from a time when boys in particular were always being prepared for some war or another. There were regularly stories about schools banning it when I was growing up, and even today you can find plenty of commentary online about its frequent prohibition. For us, the illicit thrill of something we weren't supposed to be doing was definitely one of the things that made it so exciting. Even just agreeing to play was a test of our fragile courage. Yet another opportunity, if any more were needed, for fighting without really fighting.

But looked at another way, Red Rover was also an exercise in solidarity. It required us to understand that we were all responsible for each other, that it didn't matter what strength we had individually, what mattered was the strength we had as a collective. In Red Rover, our held hands were a way to enforce a distribution of power. The game required that our strength be shared out across an entire group, making us stronger as a whole.

As we grow older, we learn that there are more meaningful uses for this knowledge than playground games. Held hands continue to be a source of collective strength. An act of resistance. In this context it is an action that is more tactical than instinctive. When marching in a protest, holding hands or linking arms is the simplest way to keep a group together. It is also, just as in Red Rover, a way of protecting that unity against violent attempts to disrupt or divide it. Young hands hold older ones. Frail hands are lent strength. The chain remains unbroken. We refuse to be moved.

Look at pictures from the Selma-to-Montgomery marches or the Greenham Common protest or the Black Lives Matter demonstrations of 2020 and you will see people holding hands and linking arms, knitting themselves together into a single body. In these contexts our held hands are the ultimate expression of our solidarity. They are quite literally what holds us together—what enables us to resist as a collective rather than as individuals. If you want to tear the prison walls down, Pete Seeger reminds us, you'll need more than one pair of hands. You'll need a million.

Keep looking at those pictures of people holding hands through a century or more of protest and the gesture itself begins to shimmer. It remains the thing that it is—a tactic, an action, a mode of behaviour—but it becomes something else also. It becomes a symbol of unified strength. It both reminds us how strong we are together and serves as a warning to those who might seek to disrupt or suppress us.

These are no longer the instinctive actions of young children or of animals. These held hands are also part of a language of gestures that we are using to communicate. They have ascended to the order of signs.

• • •

The phrase *holding hands* begins to appear in the written record in the mid-sixteenth century. It was used twice in the explorer George Best's *A True Discourse of the Late Voyages of Discoverie*, an eyewitness account of a journey through the Northwest Passage. Best uses it first to describe the width of a tree ("suche timber trees as twelve men holding handes togither are not able to fathome") and later in a description of a group of dancers upon a hill. He recalls observing a group of people "to the number of twentie in a ranke [. . .] dancing upon the hill toppes all holdyng handes over theyr heads, and dancing, with greate noyse and songs togither."

It's not totally clear that this second instance actually describes people who are holding hands as they dance, or if the individual dancers are simply holding their own hands above their heads, but for people like George Best the association between dancing and hand holding would have been a common one. Holding hands was a regular feature of dances during this period. The popular German dance the allemande, for example, involved couples slowly processing up and down the length of a ballroom, holding hands. At the same time simpler, wilder, less courtly dances, the kind George Best might be describing, were also often structured around couples holding hands. A German woodcut from the same period shows two peasant couples in bright shades of red and orange, the men with long red beards and the women wearing their hair in plaits, dancing a wild jig. Each couple have their hands clasped together and raised above their heads whilst their legs skip boisterously in time to some unheard rhythm. Beneath the illustration, an accompanying text informs the reader that one couple are happy and in love and dancing in celebration, whilst the other are busy squabbling. This is an old story, about romance and its opposite, but the reason we get the joke is because we understand, as the artist did, what it is supposed to mean to be seen dancing together in this way, hand in hand.

These dances, with their steps and their conventions, their formalised courtships, their abstraction of intimacy and desire, are an inflection point for the simple act of holding hands. With these dances, holding hands becomes a kind of performance. A gesture, an act, a pantomime even. Holding hands is now something separate to, more than, ordinary behaviour. Part of an elaborate vocabulary of human gestures—the nods and winks and waves and curtsies, the hugs and the blown kisses, the bitten thumbs and wanker gestures, this vast, fleshy syntax we use to speak silently with and about each other. It is part of the language of love, with all its subterfuge, subtext, innuendo, and slander—all the machinations of a Shakespeare comedy.

Perhaps, then, it is at this moment, in ballrooms and village squares, in George Best's dance upon a hill with all its great

noise and singing, that holding hands slips away from our animal instincts and into the human realm of discourse.

● ● ●

This seems like as good a moment as ever to mention how awkward it can often be to hold hands, one hand fumbling into and
over the other, finding the right grip—just enough of a squeeze,
but not too much, to feel like you are both holding and being
held. The slipperiness of palms varnished with nervous sweat.
Hands that are too cold or too hot, that seem to speak of two
bodies that cannot find an equilibrium. Two hands trying and
failing to come to an agreement, an unspoken negotiation that
is going off the rails.

Why does this happen? Why does holding hands sometimes
feel so easy and sometimes feel so awkward? Why does something so seemingly simple sometimes feel like it has gone so
horribly wrong?

In a 2013 study in Myrtle Beach, California, psychologists
observed that over 90 per cent of males in heterosexual romantic couples, parents in parent-child pairs, and older siblings in
child-sibling pairs tended to place their hand on top when holding hands. The psychologists concluded that holding hands in
this way was a display of social dominance. An attempt to reach
out and bend the world, or at least the person you are with, into
quiet submission.

We may not realise it, but the way we hold hands is inevitably conditioned by the social hierarchies of our culture. The

power dynamics that structure that culture inform the way we hold hands, and the way we hold hands in turn reinforces those dynamics, helping us understand who has the power in any given relationship. If you accept your place within that hierarchy, perhaps this whole process goes unnoticed, each held hand quietly reinforcing a set of relationships that you have already accepted as true and fair. But when you reject those old assumptions about who should be in charge, a held hand becomes a site of confusion, negotiation, and frequent awkwardness.

Perhaps this makes more sense of those awkward encounters, all those fumbling hands and nervous sweats. They are, to an extent, a good thing—a result of two people trying to find their own way through centuries of inherited cultural memory and social etiquette, casually whilst walking along and without saying a word to each other. Like attempting a discussion about the weather using only your eyelashes.

• • •

In my first year of secondary school, when I was twelve years old, our teachers took the whole of our year group on a week-long trip to the village of Valkenburg in the western Netherlands. We drove all the way there in two hired coaches. It was the summer of Euro 96, the European football championship, and the teachers appeared to have the same end-of-term buzz as us, standing by the coach door smoking cheap European cigarettes and drinking small green bottles of continental lager.

My concerns on the trip were twofold: to make sure I saved

enough of my spending money to buy myself a good present (I wanted a set of hand-painted ornamental wooden clogs, which I did eventually buy and which sat proudly on my windowsill at home for the next half decade or so), and to try and get Katie Joel to fall back in love with me. We had briefly gone out at the very beginning of the school year, just after we had first met. At this point, "going out" was a euphemism—we weren't actually old enough to go out anywhere, so going out consisted entirely of spending each break time walking around the school, holding hands. Katie and I were both very tiny eleven-year-olds, and so to everyone older or taller than us, which was everyone, our presence was something to be adored in loud and patronising terms. Unfortunately it hadn't worked out for Katie and me that year, but I was hoping the trip to Valkenburg might offer a second chance.

Throughout the trip, the groups of children assigned to each of the coaches were pitted against each other by the teachers in a series of almost-competitions—who behaved best, who kept their coach the cleanest, who was ready first in the morning. We consistently lost these challenges, and eventually the delight we took in doing so resulted in the teachers deciding that we needed to be collectively punished. Their chosen way of doing so was to parade us through the streets of Valkenburg, hand in hand with a classmate of the opposite sex, like four-year-olds on a nursery school day trip. This, they imagined, was the ideal humiliation for a group of eleven- and twelve-year-olds, an opportunity to make us look like the little children we all still secretly were and to force us to navigate the fraught relationship politics of whose hand to hold and what "people" would have to say about it.

We walked through the streets in our neat little line, to the amusement of our teachers and our classmates on the other coach, puppets in someone else's show, each of us reacting to this enforced charade in our own way: resentful, upset, humiliated, and quietly thrilled. Katie and I had agreed to hold hands. This was, at least, something we had experience in. And at first, at least, it was nice to imagine the assumptions that everyone else might be making about what this display of public affection meant. Quickly, however, I could tell, even if no one else could, that in reality it didn't mean anything. We held hands politely for as long as we had to, but Katie didn't love me and she never again would.

• • •

John Lennon and Paul McCartney wrote "I Want to Hold Your Hand" in the basement of Jane Asher's parents' house in London, sitting together behind a single old piano, looking across at each other and playing the keys together, "eyeball to eyeball," as John described it.

The song was released as a single in November 1963. Watch footage of the Beatles a year later, playing it live at the Washington Coliseum, and even across a distance of more than half a century you can feel the thrill of it: the screaming, the security guards patrolling the aisles, the audience all vibrating at the same urgent frequency, feeling their deepest, most unspoken longings and desires coalescing into the shape of a perfect two-and-a-half-minute pop song.

In 1963 the Beatles were little more than a generation past the complex and rigid rules of Edwardian public manners, whereby a lady never took her gloves off in public and unmarried girls of a certain class were always accompanied by a chaperone. Yet here were four boys in their early twenties, playing guitars as loudly as possible and screaming to anyone who would listen about a love they couldn't hide. It may now sound a little chaste, this neat two-part harmony, this polite request to hold someone's hand, but when they get to the part where they sing about touching you and feeling happy inside, it still contains a vivid erotic charge, pulsing with a permissiveness that feels new, thrilling, and alive. "We sing about love, but we mean sex," John had boasted a few months earlier, "and the fans know it."

"I Want to Hold Your Hand" is a song about a desire that cannot, and *should* not, be restrained. But it is also a song in which the singers are acutely aware of the double nature of the request they are making. Holding hands is something we do because it feels good—to touch, to be connected, all that muscle memory of the safety and the strength that come from holding on to someone, infused with new feelings and new desires, with love, with sex, with longing.

But it is also a gesture they know will be seen and recognised as a public declaration. To hold hands is to announce ourselves as being together romantically. To hold hands is to say that you will let me be your man.

This is, of course, a very culturally specific understanding of this gesture, an understanding that contains in its bone marrow the history of the Western Renaissance and its occasionally stiff, occasionally bawdy courtship dances. A statement that translates very differently elsewhere. In those parts of the Arabic world where the sexes are still generally segregated, men and women do not hold hands in public, but men will hold hands with each other as a show of kinship. To touch each other and to hold each other is to declare a kind of commonality, an equality of status. It signifies not two people becoming one, but rather two people in balance with each other. A different kind of devotion, perhaps, but a devotion nonetheless.

But for the Beatles, as for the twelve-year-old me in Valkenburg, holding hands is a romantic declaration. And when we are holding hands, we do so aware of its particular, historically contingent double nature, as something that just makes us feel good and a way of communicating something specific about ourselves to the world. We are both being intimate and performing intimacy. We are signifier and signified. We are speaking to each other, and we are speaking together to everybody else around us.

The ease with which the Beatles can navigate this fraught no man's land between private behaviour and public gesture, or indeed how well already at the age of twelve my classmates and I understood this same terrain, speaks to how deeply ingrained within our culture this particular gesture is.

But, of course, not everyone has the privilege of being able to move with such frictionless ease between personal desire and public expression. When "I Want to Hold Your Hand" was released in the UK, homosexuality was still illegal. The age of consent in the UK wouldn't be equalised until 2001. Section 28 of the Local Government Act, prohibiting the "promotion of homosexuality" in schools, wasn't repealed until 2003. LGBT individuals weren't given full anti-discrimination protections until the Equality Act in 2010, and weren't permitted to serve openly in the armed forces until 2016.

When love and identity are in conflict with the historic prejudices of a homophobic and transphobic society, a gesture as seemingly simple as holding hands becomes a site of fraught and contested meaning.

In Patricia Highsmith's semi-autobiographical 1952 novel *The Price of Salt*, the character of Therese describes her desire for her lover, Carol, with all the fervour of Lennon and McCartney—"I love you, I love you, I love," she says, before describing the way a brush of her foot under the table makes her go limp and tense at the same time. She thinks of the people she has seen holding hands in the movie theatre, asking herself, "Why shouldn't she and Carol? Yet when she simply took Carol's arm as they stood choosing a box of candy in a shop, Carol murmured, 'Don't.' "

Holding hands is usually an act people perform because they want to, because they need to. They feel it in their gut, that need to reach out and touch, to hold, to be held. But its history as a symbolic gesture of unity, courtship, and desire also means that when we do reach out and hold one another's hand, that gesture is read by the people around us as a declaration—a statement about ourselves. For heterosexual couples this public declaration—a *display* of affection, as it is usually, tellingly, called—is often so banal as to go unnoticed. But when who you are and who you love does not conform to your society's narrow historic conventions, there isn't the same casual synchronicity between intimate desire and public performance. Public declaration is interpreted as political statement, and suddenly a gesture that had almost disappeared in its banality becomes, sometimes almost unbearably, visible.

At the time of writing, homosexuality is illegal in sixty-seven countries. As recently as February 2021, *Pink News* reported on a homophobic attack in New Zealand—a country currently ranked fourth in the world in the Social Progress Index—on two teenagers who were surrounded by a group of around a dozen other teenagers who began yelling homophobic abuse and physically assaulting them in broad daylight because, according to one of the victim's mothers, "they were two girls holding hands."

● ● ●

Several years ago I found myself walking through the electronics department of a labyrinthine Hong Kong department store, holding hands with a complete stranger. He was maybe nineteen or twenty years old. He spoke little English and I spoke no Cantonese, so we drifted together through a forest of blinking lights and luminous screens in a silence that was constantly on the verge of slipping into awkwardness but never quite did. People watched us curiously as we passed. Or perhaps I just felt like they did. My white, male, heterosexual body so used to appearing, in Sarah Ahmed's phrase, "unmarked by strangeness" that walking hand in hand with another man through such a busy public space was to be suddenly prickled by visibility.

This walk was part of a performance by the Glasgow-based artist Rosana Cade called *Walking:Holding*. From its conception the piece was an attempt to contend with the politics of visibility in public space—the way in which certain bodies are marked by difference, those "for whom public life was not designed," as Sarah Ahmed again describes. In the performance, one audience member at a time is taken on a walk around a city, hand in hand with a series of strangers. The people the audience walk with are residents of the city who have agreed to take part in the piece, people of various ages, genders, sexualities. As you walk with each of these people in turn, you might share a conversation with them, or you might simply walk in silence. Rosana describes this experience as being able to feel—first hand—"what it is like to walk in someone else's hands."

Informed by their own experience as a queer person, Rosana understands the declarative nature of a pair of publicly held hands; the way observers read them and through them the identities of the people doing the holding. The hands you hold in *Walking:Holding* become like disguises you slip in and out of, your body more or less "marked by difference" depending on who it is that you are walking with. To take part is to become a kaleidoscope. A human mix tape shuffling from track to track.

Slowly, subtly, the intersecting obstacles and oppressions that circumscribe the way different people can move through the world are rendered temporarily visible. We walk and we hold, and this walking and holding becomes a new way of looking at the world.

The young man in the department store guided us towards the exit and we emerged near a busy intersection into muggy late-afternoon sunshine. Nearly five years later, I still carry that memory of holding his hand, holding on to a way of being—and a way of being marked—that is not mine, but that he and Rosana have so generously and tenderly leant to me.

By a set of steps another stranger was waiting to collect me, a student who would spend the next ten minutes quick-marching me across empty concrete skywalks like an errant little brother she had been given strict responsibility for, all the while telling me about her role in the democracy protests of 2014. As she did so I would feel that prickliness subside, feel myself slipping back into something approaching the privileged body and identity I have grown so comfortably familiar with.

● ● ●

In September 2020, in the teeth of the coronavirus pandemic, a team of engineering researchers from Japan's Gifu University posted a video on YouTube of their latest project. In the video a young man in a disposable face mask can be seen walking down an anonymous-looking corridor. He walks normally, except for the fact that his right arm appears to be connected to some kind of mechanical device—a clumsy assemblage of metal rods and wires attached to his bicep by a Velcro strap, ending in a white silicone hand which the man holds in his own hand, fingers interlocked.

The device is called Osampo Kanojo—or, in English, "My Girlfriend in Walk"—and according to the accompanying news article it is intended by the researchers as means for people to "experience holding your girlfriend's hand more easily than by finding a girlfriend." It is also, they claim, designed as a means to comfort people left isolated by the pandemic. A robot hand, with which to attempt to fabricate the chemical reaction in our brains that soothes us when we hold someone's hand. In another shot from the video, we see how, when pressure is applied to the palm, the silicone hand flexes slightly in response, the fingers curling gently but insistently inwards.

A great deal of care has been put into ensuring that the experience closely approximates that of holding the hand of another person. The hand itself is soft, pliable, and responsive to touch, automatically reciprocating any tightening of your grip or momentary squeeze. It has an internal heater to replicate the warmth of a human hand and releases trace amounts of water as you walk, like tiny beads of perfumed sweat moistening your entwined palms. Aware that two people holding hands are never entirely in sync with one another, the engineers have even designed a mechanism within the device that causes it to slide backwards if you start to walk too quickly, as if your partner is struggling to keep up with you. On an attached set of headphones, you can listen to a rhythmic accompaniment of footsteps, the sound of breathing, and the occasional quiet rustle of clothing.

There have been many attempts to use technology to over-come our lack of human connection during the pandemic, to varying degrees of success. Some of those technologies have been very simple, like the banging of pots and pans on doorsteps, whilst others have been relatively cutting edge: live-streamed theatre and music gigs, online pub quizzes, and virtual raves. In all these examples technology is used as a means of mediating our connection to the people around us, a way of surmounting our physical separation from one another.

The Osampo Kanojo takes a profoundly different approach to the same problem, doing away with human connection entirely in favour of its simulation. It aims to replicate the sensation of touch so meticulously that it is able to stand in for, even replace, the experience of human interaction, implying the presence of another person, when in reality it is just an echo. It is a fantasy of exteriority that instead draws us farther and farther inwards, like falling in love with someone you meet in a dream.

Is this a premonition of some dystopian future of complete social fragmentation? A world in which we exist only within our own algorithmically maintained feedback loops? A new dawn in which we are each locked in a machine embrace, just squeezing and being squeezed back forever?

Or are such experiments the harbinger of a new era of machine–human relationships, in which, as Donna Haraway might have it, "people are not afraid of their joint kinship with animals and machines"? Given what the work of artists like Rosana Cade has to show us about the empathetic power of holding hands, will we learn to love machines when they learn how to hold us?

Another study, from 2020, by the University of Electro-Communications in Tokyo, invited a group of very young children to interact with a robot in their kindergarten. A control group of children simply played with the robot for thirty minutes, whilst another group played only after they had walked across the classroom holding hands with it. Researchers found that the second group of children were more open to the robot, stating "to hold hands is to physically connect oneself with another [. . .] This kind of togetherness made the child feel that he or she and the robot were of the same species, and finally made the children feel that the robot was safe."

In the future, the study declares, "it is expected that robots will come to be recognised as friend-like entities, neither machines nor complete strangers."

• • •

What will the machines need to learn about holding hands to really be our friends?

When to hold on tightly and when not to

how tight is too tight

how tight is not tight enough

how to clutch someone's hand in the darkness of a cinema when the movie gets a little too much

how to hold them gently in the unbearable quiet of a hospital waiting room

how to warm each other's hands in the depths of a coat pocket

how to keep each other together when rough hands are trying to pull you apart

how to hold hands not as an exertion of power

but as an act of empathy

or an act of solidarity

the difference between holding hands on a busy street

and holding hands on the sofa

how to dance

boisterously or otherwise

that squeeze of the fingers that says

everything is going to be ok

or if not ok it will pass

like everything else

the slight rearrangement of the fingers

that half stroke along the back of your hand

even the way the blood moves quicker under the skin

those almost imperceptible movements

that somehow tell you everything you need to know

love probably

probably they will need to know about love

and then just about the feeling of

holding

and being held

even if only temporarily.

POSTSCRIPT

SOME THINGS TO DO WITH THIS BOOK NOW THAT YOU HAVE FINISHED READING IT

1. Give your copy to a friend or a relative or someone sitting opposite you on the train.

2. Hand this book to a passing stranger on a crowded street.

3. Hand this book to a passing stranger on an empty street, whispering to them as you do so, "Guard this with your life."

4. Or tear out all the pages and send one to each of the contacts in your phone's address book, inviting them to come together with you at a designated time and place for a collective reading.

5. Or turn each page into a paper aeroplane and see which of your friends can launch theirs the farthest.

6. Or find a seat in a crowded bar, take out this book, and pretend to be reading. Pretend to be reading when in actual fact what you are doing is listening to the conversations taking place

around you, the drunken arguments, the awkward first dates, the complicated drinks orders. Listen to the bar with the kind of concentration you would normally reserve for a piece of music.

7. Or stand up in the middle of a busy cinema pointing at a page in this book and screaming, "It's all happening just as he said it would!"

8. Or write your phone number in the front of the book and leave it in a coffee shop with instructions for the person who finds it to call you if and when they make it to the end.

9. Or leave this book in the house of someone you are besotted with but too afraid to tell in the hope that they will one day read this postscript and finally understand what you were trying to say to them.

10. Or you could read it aloud in church.

11. Or read it aloud in the club.

12. Or read it aloud from your bedroom window.

13. Or read it aloud to the strangers in the park.

14. Or read it aloud to a telemarketer.

15. Or shred all the pages and scatter them like confetti over the people you love.

There are many things you could do with this book now. But whatever you choose to do with it, do it with care.

ACKNOWLEDGEMENTS

There are many people to thank for the existence of this book, but the first should be my friend Amber Massie Blomfield, who patiently held my hand through the earliest stages of turning this half-formed idea into thousands of actual words. That process also required the kindness and support of all the members of our writers group, in particular Cailey Rizzo, Kirsty Sedgman, Kate Wyver, and Georgie Codd, all of whom taught me things about writing books that I didn't know before.

I feel incredibly fortunate to be represented by Emma Bal, whose dizzying enthusiasm and improbable belief in this book were a huge part in making it real, and to have had as my editors Alane Mason and Hannah MacDonald, who understood what I was trying to say and showed me how to say it so much better.

Thank you to Maddy Costa, my regular writing partner and friend, without whom I never would have thought a project like this was possible, and to Deborah Pearson for the seventeen years of artistic collaboration that have shaped the way I think about the world. Thank you also to my mum and dad, who continue to teach me what real care looks like.

All the artists whose work I mention in this book are weird and brilliant and deserve more space than I was able to give them: Darren O'Donnell, Nando Messias, Jenny Hunt and Holly Darton, Rimini Protokoll, Charlotte Jarvis, Abigail Conway, Britt Hatzius, Briony Campbell, Rosana Cade, and Ira Brand. Do seek out their work if you can. A special mention as well to the many young people I have worked with—in St Helens, São Paulo, Manchester, and elsewhere—whose ideas about the world this book is soaked in.

Thank you to my hairdresser, Susana, for the haircuts and the stories about her pigeons. Thank you to Tom Parkinson for explaining patiently how to describe music properly, and to Christopher Brett Bailey for being an excellent moviegoing companion. Thank you to Ali Litherland for her quiet acts of call-centre resistance and to my brother for his late-night phone calls and much more besides.

A significant amount of the writing of this book was done with the oblivious support of Sausage the dog, whose contribution to my life is immeasurable. One of his best contributions was to introduce me to Rebekah Lattin-Rawstrone (and her dog Bessie) and Peta-Megan Dunn (and her dog Ripley), who have been an invaluable source of advice throughout the writing process.

ACKNOWLEDGEMENTS

Thank you also to all the strangers I have sheltered from the rain with and all of the strangers I have argued in the park with. Thank you to the bodies on the dance floor and the screams in the movie theatre. Thank you to everyone whose hand I have ever held, out of love or solidarity or fear.

Thank you most of all to Beckie, for every small act of kindness and support that enabled me to write this book, and for all the encounters we have had together—the nights of dancing, the Zoom calls, the phone calls, the dog walks, the road trips, the moments of euphoria, and the spaces in between. Thank you for being exactly as excited by and afraid of the world as I am.

NOTES ON SOURCES

This book wouldn't exist without the work of Georges Perec, in particular *Species of Spaces and Other Pieces* and *An Attempt at Exhausting a Place in Paris*, both of which provided me with a blueprint for the way writing can illuminate the obvious and the overlooked, rendering visible that which had become invisible to us.

The Importance of Care

The key sources for this chapter were *Hair: A Human History* by Kurt Stenn, *Hair Story: Untangling the Roots of Black Hair in America* by Ayana Byrd and Lori Tharps, and Victoria Sherrow's *Encyclopedia of Hair: A Cultural History*.

David L Shabazz's essay "Barbershops as Cultural Forums for African American Males" in the *Journal of Black Studies* (May 2016) was enormously helpful as a starting point for thinking about the value and importance of the African American barbershop in cultural life. I would recommend seeking out all of Steve James's documentary series about Chicago, *City So Real*, both for its barbershops and the hundred careful portraits it paints of the people who call that city home.

The survey of UK women I reference was carried out in 2013 by the website NetVoucherCodes.co.uk, which asked 360 women about their relationship with their hairdresser, over half of whom described it as one of the ten most important relationships in their life. Amongst these women the average length of their relationship with a hairdresser was twelve and a half years, longer than the average failed marriage in the UK.

The description of Nat "The Bush Doctor" Mathis and his salon is drawn from a brief, but I think completely wonderful, clip uploaded to YouTube by Edward Coker (https://youtu.be/yDb8rtnnu8M). At the time I'm writing this it has been watched a grand total of sixty-six times.

Six Small Interruptions

I first encountered the work of Juliana Schroeder and Nicholas Epley in Joe Keohane's excellent book *The Power of Strangers: The Benefits of Connecting in a Suspicious World*, which was a key source for thinking about our sometimes-fraught relationships with the strangers around us. In writing about Diane Arbus, I relied upon Patricia Bosworth's great biography of Arbus, *Diane Arbus: A Biography*, and Hilton Als' truly wonderful essay "The Art of Difference" in the *New York Review of Books* (June 8, 2017).

The horrified responses to the London Underground "tube chat" badges were culled from the #tube_chat hashtag on Twitter and Jamie Grierson's September 29, 2016, article in the *Guardian*, " 'Tube chat' campaign provokes horror among London commuters."

The key source on begging was *Begging Questions: Street-Level Economic Activity and Social Policy Failure*, edited by Hartley Dean, in particular Bill Jordan's chapter, "Begging: the global context and international comparisons."

John Updike's essay "Spring Rain" (published in the April 21, 1962, issue) can be found in the archives of *The New Yorker*. My descriptions of medieval London wreathed in ice owe much to Alexandra Harris's glorious book *Weatherland: Writers and Artists Under English Skies*. My own description of a snowball fight in East London borrows from an earlier self-published short essay about this same event.

Maarten Koeners's ideas around play can be explored in his and Joseph Francis's 2020 article "The Physiology of Play: Potential Relevance for Higher Education" in the *International Journal of Play*.

More about the incredible work of both Nando Messias and Hunt and Darton can be found on their respective websites—nandomessias.com and huntanddarton.com.

A Short History of Not Going Out

I first heard about Myrna Kurland thanks to a Twitter thread by writer Arabelle Sicardi (@arabellesicardi) which sent me scurrying back to Marie Cartier's original book *Baby, You Are My Religion: Women, Gay Bars, and Theology Before Stonewall* for the full story.

I'd strongly recommend reading Ian Bogost's full article in the *Atlantic* about our changing telephone habits, "Don't Hate the Phone Call, Hate the Phone" (August 2015).

The statistic that 81 per cent of call centre workers have experienced customer abuse comes from a September 10, 2021, article in the Indian newspaper the *Business Standard*, "36% of Call Centre Agents Have Been Threatened with Violence: Study."

You can read Jules and Michael Verne's short story "In the Year 2889" in full at Project Gutenberg (https://www.gutenberg.org/files/19362/193 62-h/19362-h.htm).

Key sources on the 1964 World's Fair were Richard Barbrook's essay "New York Prophecies: The Imaginary Future of Artificial Intelligence" from the June 2007 issue of *Science as Culture* and Iain A. Boal's 2008 *Mute* magazine article "Falling for the Future."

The full story of the Bell Labs Picturephone is told in Sarah Laskow's September 2014 article for the *Atlantic*, "The First 'Picturephone' for Video Chatting Was a Colossal Failure."

The Apple product launch I describe at length in this chapter is the 2010 launch event for the iPhone 4. You can watch the entire launch, as I did, on YouTube (https://youtu.be/z__jxoczNWc).

A Home You Can Carry with You

The performance I describe that took place in a parked car was called *Motor Vehicle Sundown* (in homage to a George Brecht artwork of the same name). You can experience this piece yourself for free by following the instructions on the project's Soundcloud page (https://on.soundcloud .com/CMr7).

According to the US Centers for Disease Control and Prevention website, there were 40,698 motor vehicle traffic deaths in the United States in 2020 and 45,222 firearms deaths (https://www.cdc.gov/nchs/fastats/ accidental-injury.htm). Until very recently motor vehicle traffic deaths still outnumbered firearms deaths, but, as reported by *Scientific American* in May 2022 ("Guns Now Kill More Children and Young Adults than Car Crashes"), traffic deaths have been consistently falling in the last two decades whilst firearms deaths in the same period have only continued to rise.

The link between eye contact and cognitive processing comes from research by Shogo Kajimura and Michio Nomura from Kyoto University in their 2016 paper in the journal *Cognition*, "When We Cannot Speak: Eye Contact Disrupts Resources Available to Cognitive Control Processes During Verb Generation."

The figure of ten Hyde Parks as the amount of space taken up by on-street parking comes from a March 2020 article by researcher Joe Wills on the website *City Monitor* (https://citymonitor.ai/environment/london-s-street-parking-takes-much-space-10-hyde-parks-4972).

Society in Six Meals

Two key texts that informed my thinking about our relationship to food were *Eating Together*, by Alice P. Julier and Katie Rawson, and Elliott Shore's *Dining Out: A Global History of Restaurants*. I also spent a lot of time listening to the wonderful podcasts *Lecker* by Lucy Dearlove (https://www.leckerpodcast.com) and *Proof* from America's Test Kitchen (https://www.americastestkitchen.com/podcasts/proof).

The description of the *lazzaroni* of Naples was drawn primarily from Antonio Mattozzi's fascinating book *Inventing the Pizzeria: A History of Pizza Making in Naples*.

I read far too many articles about the Surrealist Ball, the majority of which regurgitated the same few facts next to the same images of Audrey Hepburn and Salvador Dalí, but the one that I found most helpful was "Party Animals: The Rothschild Surrealist Ball" by Ed Cripps in *The Rake* in December 2016.

My key source on food sharing in primates was the helpfully titled chapter "Food-Sharing in Primates: A Critical Review" by Anna T. C. Feistner and W. C. McGrew in *Perspectives in Primate Biology, vol. 3*.

More of Robin Dunbar's ideas around the importance of social relationships can be found in his excellent book *Friends: Understanding the Power of Our Most Important Relationships*, which was helpful not just for this chapter but across the whole of this book.

Ecstatic Escape

In describing Congo Square I relied upon Jerah Johnson's article "New Orleans's Congo Square: An Urban Setting for Early Afro-American Culture Formation" in the spring 1991 issue of the journal *Louisiana History*.

Some key sources on the history of Chicago house and Detroit techno were "Post-soul Futurama: African American Cultural Politics and Early Detroit Techno" by Sean Albiez in the *European Journal of American Culture* (August 2005); "Beyond the Hood? Detroit Techno, Underground Resistance, and African American Metropolitan Identity Politics" by Christopher Schaub, published in the October 2009 issue of the journal *Forum for Inter-American Research*; and Jacob Arnold's history of the Warehouse, "The Warehouse: The Place House Music Got Its Name," for *Resident Advisor* (published in May 2012 and available at https://jp.ra.co/features/1597). You can listen to the wild story of the rise and fall of Manchester's Hacienda nightclub told by the people that helped create it on the brilliant podcast *Transmissions: The Definitive Story of Joy Division and New Order* (https://podcasts.apple.com/gb/podcast/transmissions-the-definitive-story-of-joy-division/id1534628327).

Yuko Hattori's research is outlined in an article she co-wrote with Masaki Tomonaga for the *Proceedings of the National Academy of Sciences* (January 2020) entitled "Rhythmic Swaying Induced by Sound in Chimpanzees."

The quotation from Simone Weil was found in "Beyond Rhythmanalysis: Towards a Territoriology of Rhythms and Melodies in Everyday Spatial Activities" by Andrea Mubi Brighenti and Mattias Kärrholm (published in *City, Territory and Architecture* in 2018), whilst Jamie Principe's description of going to the Power Plant comes from a June 2016 *Vice* article by Alex Frank, "The Story of Jamie Principle and Frankie Knuckles' 'Your Love,' the Sexiest Dance Cut of All Time" (https://www.vice.com/en/article/d7jxzv/jamie-principle-frankie-knuckles-your-love).

A special thank you to my partner, Beckie, whose effortless cool guided us serenely past the bouncers and up into the dark and booming heart of Berghain.

A Great Green Emptiness at the Centre of Everything

The full story of the creation of the UK's first public parks is entertainingly told in *A Walk in the Park: The Life and Times of a People's Institution* by Travis

Elborough, whilst Rubika Shah's film *White Riot* is an excellent introduction to Rock Against Racism, featuring the fantastic footage I describe of the Clash performing in Victoria Park.

The prices of AEG's All Points East Festival refer to the 2021 edition of the event.

The research on dogs and sociability I reference from the University of Warwick is detailed in "Dogs as Catalysts for Social Interactions: Robustness of the Effect" by June McNicholas and Glyn M. Collis in the *British Journal of Psychology* (February 2000). Equally important for my thinking on dogs was Donna Haraway's *Companion Species Manifesto: Dogs, People, and Significant Otherness*, in which she describes beautifully the "joint dance of being" that dogs and their owners undertake together as they learn from and with each other.

Richard Sennett has written extensively about the urban landscape, but the book I most relied on here was *Building and Dwelling: Ethics for the City*. Also valuable was Dan Hancox's writing on public space in the *Guardian*, in particular his July 5, 2019, piece "Revealed: Creeping Privatisation of London Parks in Summer" and "The Power of Crowds" (June 2, 2020).

Space to Dream

Some key sources on early cinema were Stuart Hanson's *From Silent Screen to Multi-screen: A History of Cinema Exhibition in Britain Since 1896*, James Chapman's *Cinemas of the World: Film and Society from 1895 to the Present*, and Charlotte Herzog's 1984 article "The Archaeology of Cinema Architecture: The Origins of the Movie Theater" in the *Quarterly Review of Film Studies*. In terms of the more recent history of moviegoing culture, Stephen Hunter's introduction to his essay collection *Now Playing at the Valencia* provided an invaluable example of the way different cinemas create their own microcultures.

Another huge influence on this chapter was the writing of Julian Hanich, in particular his book *Cinematic Emotion in Horror Films and Thrillers: The Aesthetic Paradox of Pleasurable Fear* and his articles "Watching a Film with Others: Towards a Theory of Collective Spectatorship" in the journal *Screen* (Autumn 2014) and "Laughter and Collective Awareness: The Cinema Auditorium as Public Space" in the journal *NECSUS—European Journal of Media Studies* (Autumn 2014). It was through Hanich that I discovered the wonderful André Bazin and Pauline Kael quotes that are included in this chapter.

You can read more about Claes Oldenburg's strange and extraordinary *Moveyhouse* in *Raw Notes*, an exhaustive compendium of notes and scripts from some of his early, brilliant performance works. Whilst I was writing this chapter and Oldenburg's work was again present in my thoughts (as it so often is), it was announced that he had died at the age of ninety-three, and so I would like to dedicate this chapter to him.

The Simple Pleasure of Holding Hands

The paper "Lending a Hand: Social Regulation of the Neural Response to Threat" in the journal *Psychological Science* (December 2016) outlines the experiment I describe into the impact of holding hands on our response to threatening stimuli.

The reference to holding hands in the writing of George Best I discovered thanks to Peter Lukas, an editor at the website ElizabethanDrama.org, who was responding to a question about the origin of the phrase *holding hands* on Quora.

The quote from John Lennon comes from Craig Brown's masterful book *One Two Three Four: The Beatles in Time,* which also describes the writing of "I Want to Hold Your Hand." The phrase "unmarked by strangeness" comes from Sara Ahmed's book *Strange Encounters: Embodied Others in Post-Coloniality.* The figure for the number of countries where homosexuality is still illegal comes from the August 2022 *Newsweek* article by Giulia Carbonaro, "Homosexuality Is Still Illegal in These 67 UN Countries" (https://www.newsweek.com/homosexuality-illegal-67-un-countries-1735575).

In thinking about holding hands with robots I drew from Donna Haraway's *Cyborg Manifesto* and its imagining of a future in which the categories of human and robot begin to bleed into one another.

Finally, the text that concludes this chapter is primarily taken from *put your sweet hand in mine,* a 2015 performance I co-wrote and performed in with the artist Ira Brand. The show took place in a long, narrow space in which two rows of audience members sat facing one another. At the end of the show they were invited to reach out in the darkness and hold the hand of the stranger opposite them, whilst Ira read a version of this text. The full script for the performance can be found in the book *Forest Fringe: The First Ten Years.*